Vegetable Cooking

Author: Annette Wolter
Photography: Rolf Feuz and Karin Messerli
Translated by UPS Translations, London
Edited by Josephine Bacon

CLB 4180
This edition published in 1995 by Colour Library Books Ltd
Published originally under the title "Brot und Herzhaftes Gebäck"
by Gräfe und Unzer Verlag GmbH, München
© 1995 Gräfe und Unzer Verlag GmbH, München
English translation copyright: © 1995 by
Colour Library Books Ltd, Godalming, Surrey
Typeset by Image Setting, Brighton, E. Sussex
Printed and bound in Singapore
ISBN 1-85833-315-6

VEGETABLE COOKING

Annette Wolter

Contributors
Elke Alsen, Marey Kurz,
Annedore Meineke and Brigitta Stuber

Photography
Rolf Feuz and Karin Messerli

CLB
Colour Library Books

Contents

Special Vegetable Dishes

Vegetables from A to Z

Index

About this Book

Fresh vegetables are one of the most attractive aspects of the art of cooking, and are an inexhaustible source of inspiration to the creative cook. Vegetable cookery is favoured by the huge range of native as well as more exotic varieties available in shops throughout the year.

In recent years, through experience of eating abroad and through sampling dishes prepared by our own ethnic communities, we have also learnt how superb and diverse vegetables can be if they are properly prepared. Another reason for their growing popularity is the high nutritional value of vegetables. They are rich in vitamins and minerals, but very low in calories.

Delicious vegetable fare! This beautifully produced cookery book, with colour illustrations throughout, tells you how to create the most delicious vegetable dishes. Just glancing through the superb colour photographs – every recipe is illustrated – shows how richly varied vegetable cookery can be. You will find not only familiar, popular dishes such as stuffed peppers or stuffed cabbage leaves, but also tempting ways of preparing vegetables that are not so well known, such as vegetable soufflés, pickled vegetables, vegetables combined with fish or poultry, satisfying vegetable bakes and delicious purées served as an attractive accompaniment. Recipes include a Swiss chard flan, a courgette quiche and an artichoke pizza.

To make sure you get full value from the vegetables you eat, the first pages of the book are devoted to telling you what to look for when you go shopping. Then comes a description of the best methods of cooking vegetables, illustrated with clear, step-by-step photographs that are easy to follow. The range of the recipes described makes it easy to find a suitable dish for every occasion and to experiment with new ideas. The book is set out in a way that makes it easy to use.

In the first chapter you will find delicious vegetable soups, hors d'oeuvres and light meals. As well as familiar soups like bean or potato soup, you will also find, for example, a recipe for minestrone – the classic Italian soup – or a delicate sorrel soup (sorrel is now becoming more widely available commercially). Such classic hors d'oeuvres as Waldorf salad or stuffed artichokes alternate with exquisite surprises such as Swiss chard au gratin or grilled avocados.

You will be surprised by the diversity on offer in the chapter on main courses. Sometimes vegetables are combined with meat, fish or poultry, but there are many nutritious, delectable recipes without any of these additions. Here you will find the classic way of serving asparagus, popular potato dishes, stuffed vegetables, vegetables served au gratin, fritters, stuffed leaves and dishes with herbs, fennel and pumpkin. Stews, hotpots and baked vegetable dishes with a very wide range of flavours complete this section. There are also recipes for varieties of vegetables that are less widely available such as cardoon, okra or Jerusalem artichokes. Vegetarians will be delighted with the culinary treats on offer.

Of course there are also many suggestions in the book for vegetable salads and attractive accompaniments for those who want to eat vegetables every day in some form or other, while continuing to have fish, meat or poultry as their main course. The selection takes you through every season of the year, bearing in mind varieties that are available constantly as imports. In salads, vegetables are naturally used raw as much as possible. All these side dishes taste so good that you will happily cut down on your usual big helping of meat to eat more of them.

The section on 'Special Vegetable Dishes' offers traditional dishes from many lands. For example, there is borscht from Russia, choucroûte from Alsace, ratatouille from the Mediterranean, chili con carne from Mexico or Turkish aubergine stew. These are followed by filling pastry dishes such as pizzas or quiches, delicious to serve to your friends and guests with beer and wine.

The marvellous photographs make it easier to choose. All the recipes are clearly described in uncomplicated terms so that even inexperienced cooks can re-create them successfully. Below the list of ingredients in every recipe there is information about preparation and cooking times and advice on how nutritious it is. This makes it easier to plan meals sensibly.

In the final section of the book you will find descriptions on double-page spreads framed by colourful illustrations of all the varieties of vegetables for which this book provides recipes. The nutrients and minerals in which each variety is especially rich are given here; you are told which spices or herbs go particularly well with them, and which vegetables combine best with one another. The seasons for harvesting vegetables grown out-of-doors are given, as are tips on storing them correctly.

Unless otherwise stated, all recipes are for four people.

The Value of Vegetables

Vegetables taste good, provide vital nutrients and enrich our meals. But like all foodstuffs with a high nutritional value they suffer if handled incorrectly. You will enjoy their value to the full only if you are very selective when you buy, and treat them with care afterwards.

A perfect shape, large size and a gleaming surface are no guarantee of quality. Nowadays such aesthetic appeal can often be achieved by using chemical fertilisers and treatments, which may leave unwholesome residues in the plants. When you are shopping look for vegetables that are grown as near as possible to where you live. Vegetables that have ripened in the sun have their own special flavour and a typical shape and colour; they feel crisp, firm or springy as the case may be. If you can buy organically grown vegetables, do so. This type of produce is cultivated largely without the use of mineral fertilisers and chemical pesticides or fungicides. You will find information on the special characteristics you should look for in the different varieties of vegetables in the A-Z section at the back of the book. This will also tell you when native vegetables are in season, and so should be available in the shops. It is a good idea to prepare what you need for the day as soon as you have done your shopping.

The first step in preparing vegetables is cleaning them, i.e. removing earth-covered roots and any part of the plant that will not be used, such as the damaged outer leaves of a head of cabbage and the tough, dark-green leaf ends of leeks.

To get rid of any residues of lead, vegetables which have been roughly cleaned should then be thoroughly rinsed in warm running water - tender leaf vegetables should be washed in slow-running water and turned

frequently. Vegetables with a smooth skin should be rubbed well as they are rinsed. Rough surfaces with bits of soil clinging to them should be scrubbed thoroughly under warm, running water.

Pick over leaf vegetables and herbs, discarding coarse stems and damaged leaves. Scrape or peel root vegetables such as carrots, turnips or celeriac with a sharp knife or thinly peel them depending on the nature of the surface. Remove the thin fibrous outer membrane from asparagus or celery.

Skin tomatoes and peppers. Place tomatoes briefly in boiling water before peeling. Put peppers into a very hot oven or under the grill for a short time until the skin begins to split and brown.

Prepare vegetables for cooking by cutting out or pulling off any parts that cannot be eaten such as stalks or roots and coarse fibres and ribs. Do not wash the vegetables again or leave them in water after doing this; every cut you make enables valuable nutrients to be leached out.

Far more vegetables can be eaten raw than is generally realised. As their nutritional value is highest when they are eaten raw, dieticians recommend that as many vegetables as possible should be eaten raw, as salads. But this is not to everyone's taste. Many people prefer their vegetables cooked. When cooking them, you should always bear the following principles in mind:
• Always cook vegetables for as short a time as possible with just enough heat; even when cooked, vegetables should still be slightly crunchy.
• Never keep vegetables warm. If possible prepare just the right amount so that there are no leftovers. If it is unavoidable, reheat vegetables that have cooled briefly, but never do this with spinach. If spinach is reheated it becomes unwholesome, and can be positively harmful to children.
• Leave about a third of the vegetables raw to chop finely or grate, then mix these into the cooked vegetables. One exception is green beans. They cannot be eaten raw, and need to cook for 10 minutes at about 100°C/212°F for the indigestible phasein to be broken down. When serving beans - or any other cooked

vegetable - you can compensate for the nutrients lost in cooking by using fresh herbs. Chop the herbs just before you are about to serve the dish and sprinkle them over the vegetables.

Which method of cooking is best? You should always cook vegetables with very little liquid and/or fat, especially if the liquid is retained as part of the completed dish. There are a few types of vegetable that are usually boiled, like asparagus for instance; the lightly-salted cooking water can then be used for making soup. You will find suitable methods of cooking vegetables on the following pages. They are interchangeable. The method you choose will depend purely on the end result you want to achieve.

In cooking vegetables, remember the advantages of using a pressure cooker. Vegetables cook in next to no time under pressure. If you cook this way, you can omit salt, flavouring the vegetables with wine, spices or herbs, which in turn produce a delicious sauce.

Methods for Cooking Vegetables

Blanching

Brief preliminary cooking, or even complete cooking, in boiling water to which salt or lemon juice has been added. Leaf vegetables can be cooked in this way, and whole cabbage leaves are easier to roll and stuff after blanching. After the vegetables have been added, the blanching time is calculated from the time when the water returns to the boil. Depending on the quantity of vegetables immersed and their consistency the water may go off the boil when they are added. You may need to blanch vegetables in several batches.

To make a white cabbage salad, discard the outer leaves and cut the cabbage into quarters. Cut out the stem, and shred the cabbage quarters into thin, even slices, or use a slicer.

Frying

Cooking quickly in hot, preferably non-saturated vegetable fat or oil in a frying-pan. Following the recipe instructions, cut the vegetables up into small pieces of equal size. Vegetables with a high moisture content should first be dipped in flour or a light coating of breadcrumbs. If vegetables are cooked in breadcrumbs, the cooking liquid should be drained off; a spicy sauce should be offered instead.

The prepared vegetables should be patted dry with a tea-towel. If, for example, you want to make a Chinese dish, slice the vegetables into thin, regular strips.

Steaming

Cooking in a colander or vegetable steamer over boiling water. Pressure cookers are ideal for steaming, allowing the vegetables to cook under hermetically sealed conditions. The food being cooked must not come into contact with the water below, and the lid must fit as tightly as possible. As nutrients will still be absorbed into the boiling liquid, use this for a sauce or soup.

Put about 3cm/1¼ inches water in a saucepan and bring to the boil. If cooking cauliflower do not add salt, as saline steam causes the florets to discolour.

Conservative Method

Cooking over a low heat in a small quantity of fat and liquid. The liquid may be produced by the food being cooked, e.g. from vegetables with a high moisture content such as many of the leaf vegetables, mushrooms, tomatoes, courgettes or onions. When using this method try to avoid lifting the lid. Move the contents around by shaking the saucepan. Only add liquid during cooking if absolutely necessary - possibly if you are cooking larger quantities of vegetables.

Using a wide-bottomed, heavy-based saucepan, sauté diced onions, garlic and French beans in a small quantity of hot oil for about 3 minutes, turning constantly.

Using a large saucepan, bring a generous amount of salted water to the boil. Put the cabbage in a colander or vegetable steamer, and submerge it in the boiling water. Blanch for 5 minutes, counting from when the water returns to the boil.

Drain briefly, plunge the cabbage, still in the colander, into a prepared bowl of iced water, then drain thoroughly, squeezing out excess moisture if necessary. Continue as instructed in the recipe.

Heat oil in a wok or large frying-pan. First fry the garlic, ginger and onions.

Add the remaining vegetables, and fry for 6-10 minutes, turning constantly. Then season and finish the vegetables as instructed in the recipe.

Place the cauliflower in the colander with the florets facing upwards, and quickly cover the pan. Cook for 20-25 minutes; if using a pressure cooker, for 12-16 minutes.

Keep the cauliflower warm, and use the cooking liquid to make a cream sauce. Pour this round the cauliflower and, if you like, sprinkle breadcrumbs browned in butter over the top.

Pour a little hot vegetable stock into the saucepan, cover and cook the beans for 10-15 minutes, depending on their size and quantity. Move them around by shaking the saucepan.

Check once or twice to see if there is enough cooking liquid in the pan, and if there is not, add a little extra hot stock. Serve the beans scattered with freshly chopped herbs.

Methods for Cooking Vegetables

Au Gratin

Putting a finishing touch to vegetables that are already cooked, though sometimes this method is also used for cooking in its own right, as in the dish described here, Potato au Gratin. Cooking and/or browning takes place in an ovenproof dish in a hot oven. Cream, crème fraîche, double cream or cheese with dabs of butter, or a light butter sauce are spread over the surface of the dish to produce a crust.

To make Potato au Gratin, slice peeled potatoes very thinly and arrange in overlapping layers in a greased ovenproof dish, seasoning each layer with salt and pepper. Pour just enough slightly-salted boiling milk over the potatoes barely to cover them. Cook in the oven for 40 minutes at 220°C/430°F/Gas Mark 7.

Grilling

Cooking through exposure to powerful radiant heat over charcoal, under an electric grill, in an oven fitted with a grill, or in a grill-pan. Coat the food to be grilled with seasoned oil. Vegetables that are easily damaged should be grilled in greased aluminium foil; also, always wrap vegetables in cooking foil when grilling over charcoal.

Halve unpeeled aubergines lengthways, and sprinkle lemon juice over the cut surface so that the flesh does not discolour.

Boiling

Cooking in plenty of liquid. Depending on the texture of the food being cooked, the water should boil fiercely or barely simmer. If some of the cooking liquid is to be used as a sauce, cook in an open saucepan so that some of it can evaporate during cooking. If it is not required for the dish you are preparing, it can be used for soup, as it derives nutrients from the vegetables being boiled.

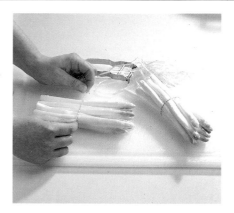

Tie prepared asparagus into bundles of about 10 stems. (Bundles are easier to lift out of the saucepan). Using a big enough saucepan or a special asparagus cooker, bring plenty of water to the boil, adding salt, a pinch of sugar and a few drops of oil.

Braising

First brown in a small quantity of hot fat. Then pour about 2cm/³/₄ inch of boiling liquid round the food to be braised, and cook in a covered saucepan, starting at a high heat which is then reduced. The braising liquid is always served as a sauce, which may be thickened and enhanced by the addition of cream, crème fraîche, double cream, wine and spices.

Pare the middle ribs from two or three blanched cabbage leaves so that they are flat. Lay them flat, and divide the filling among them. Fold over the edges of the leaves, and form into rolls.

Take the dish out of the oven, pour a mixture of egg and cream over the potatoes, top with a generous layer of grated cheese (Gruyère), and place dabs of butter at frequent intervals over the cheese. Cook for another 10 minutes until the gratin topping is golden-brown.

Check that the topping does not become too brown during cooking. If necessary cover with aluminium foil or greaseproof paper to prevent excessive browning.

Lay each half on a piece of aluminium foil large enough to cover it, sprinkle liberally with seasoned oil, wrap in the foil and leave in the refrigerator for 1½-2 hours to marinate.

Place the foil-wrapped aubergines in a very hot grill-pan, the cut surface facing downwards. Grill for 8 minutes, turn, and grill for another 8 minutes. Turn off the heat, then open the foil, and allow the cut surface to brown a little directly on the pan bottom in the residual heat.

Lower the asparagus into the boiling water. The water should be kept barely on the boil. Depending on how thick the stems are, cook for 15 to 20 minutes, covered.

Test a stem with a knife to see if the asparagus is cooked. When the knife penetrates easily the asparagus is ready. Allow the bundle of asparagus to drain on several layers of absorbent kitchen paper.

Use kitchen thread to tie up the rolls like little parcels to prevent them from opening during braising. Put about 2 tbsps oil in a saucepan or a large frying-pan with a lid.

Turn the rolls in the hot oil until they begin to brown on all sides, add the hot liquid, and braise in a covered saucepan for about 30 minutes until cooked.

Soups, Starters and Light Meals

Vegetables for every occasion.
Tried and trusted recipes,
and new discoveries

Sorrel Soup

Delicate yet sharp, to whet the appetite

Sweetcorn Soup with Peas

Delicious and satisfying

3 spring onions

400g/14oz floury potatoes

750ml/1¼ pints vegetable stock

1 tbsp oil

200g/7oz young sorrel leaves

1 large kohlrabi

4 tbsps chopped chervil

Pinch each of salt and white pepper

4 tbsps single cream

1 egg yolk

Preparation time: 10 minutes
Cooking time: 25 minutes
Nutritional value:

Analysis per serving, approx:
• 905kJ/215kcal
• 9g protein
• 8g fat
• 26g carbohydrate

Trim roots and any damaged leaves from the spring onions. Wash, dry and cut into thin rings. Peel, wash and dice the potatoes. • Heat the vegetable stock. • Heat the oil in a large saucepan, and fry the onions until transparent. Add the potatoes, pour the hot stock over them, cover and simmer for 20 minutes. • Meanwhile, wash the sorrel leaves, pick them over, drain well, and chop roughly. Peel the kohlrabi; wash the feathery green leaves. Drain well, chop finely and add to the chervil. Grate the peeled kohlrabi. • When the potatoes have cooked for 20 minutes, add the sorrel and grated kohlrabi and simmer for another 5 minutes. The potatoes should by now be disintegrating. • Season to taste. Beat the cream with the egg yolk, then stir a few tablespoons of soup into the mixture. • Remove the soup from the heat and stir in the egg-and-cream mixture. Sprinkle with the chervil before serving.

500g/1lb 2oz peas in the pod

½ tsp salt

1 l/1¾ pints water

400g/14oz canned sweetcorn

2 tsps cornflour

1 tsp sweet paprika

4 tbsps crème fraîche

4 tbsps chopped chives

Preparation time: 30 minutes
Cooking time: 5 minutes
Nutritional value:

Analysis per serving, approx:
• 880kJ/210Kcal
• 8g protein
• 6g fat
• 30g carbohydrate

Shell the peas. • Wash the pods, drain and cook them, covered, in the salted water for 20 minutes. • Purée the corn in a liquidizer or food processor with the liquid from the can or rub it through a sieve. • Drain the pea-pods, reserving the cooking water in a saucepan. • Cook the peas in the reserved liquid for 5 minutes. Add the puréed sweetcorn and more water if required and return to the boil. • Mix the cornflour and paprika with a little cold water. Thicken the soup with this mixture and finally add the crème fraîche. Sprinkle with the chives before serving.

Our Tip: French beans or strips of sweet pepper may be used instead of peas. In this case, use vegetable stock as a base.

Cream of Green Asparagus Soup

A treat for yourself, your family or your friends

1¹/₂kg/3lbs 6oz fresh asparagus
¹/₂ tsp salt
Pinch of sugar
250ml/9 fl oz vegetable stock
¹/₄ tsp white pepper
1 tbsp cornflour
100g/4oz crème fraîche
2 tbsps finely chopped fresh dill

Preparation time: 15 minutes
Cooking time: 15 minutes
Nutritional value:
Analysis per serving, approx:
• 820kJ/195kcal
• 9g protein
• 10g fat
• 16g carbohydrate

Wash and dry the asparagus. Pare away part of the lower white part of the stalks and discard the ends if woody.• Cut 5cm/2-inch lengths from the tips and set these aside.• Chop the rest of the stems into small pieces and place in a saucepan with the salt and sugar. Barely cover with water, and cook for 15 minutes in a covered pan.• Bring the vegetable stock to the boil. Add the asparagus tips, and simmer covered for 8 minutes.• Blend the pieces of stem and their cooking water in a liquidizer or food processor, or push through a sieve.• Drain the tips in a colander, reserving the stock. Combine the stock with the puréed asparagus. Season the soup with pepper and salt if required.• Mix the cornflour with a little cold water and use to thicken the soup. Finally, add the crème fraîche. Place the asparagus tips in the soup and reheat briefly.• Sprinkle with dill before serving.

Our Tip: For a more filling soup, add thin strips of smoked ham.

Cream of Tomato Soup

Aromatic herbs give this classic soup an Italian flavour

1¹/₂ kg/3lbs 6oz beefsteak tomatoes
2 onions
1 clove garlic
2 tbsps olive oil
¹/₄ tsp salt
¹/₄ tsp black pepper
¹/₂ tsp sweet paprika
1 tbsp freshly chopped mixed herbs (basil, oregano, thyme, rosemary, etc.)
¹/₂ tsp sugar
250ml/8 fl oz vegetable stock
4 tbsps sour cream
4 tbsps freshly grated Parmesan

Preparation time: 20 minutes
Cooking time: 15 minutes
Nutritional value:
Analysis per serving, approx:
• 840kJ/200kcal
• 9g protein
• 10g fat
• 18g carbohydrate

Wash and dry the tomatoes, discard the stalk ends and chop finely. Peel the onions and garlic and chop finely. • Heat the oil in a large saucepan. Gently fry the onion and garlic until transparent. • Stir in the chopped tomato, salt, pepper, paprika, herbs and sugar. Simmer, covered, over a very low heat for 15 minutes, stirring from time to time and taking care that the vegetables do not burn. Add a little vegetable stock if necessary. • Heat the stock, add to the tomatoes, then push through a fine sieve. Bring the soup back to the boil and cook for 2 minutes. Serve in individual bowls with 1 tbsp sour cream and a sprinkling of Parmesan cheese.

Our Tip: When buying beefsteak tomatoes, choose very ripe ones as they have the best flavour.

Cucumber Soup with Dill

A smooth consistency, and a fresh taste

1kg/2¹/₄lbs cucumber
1 tsp fresh (or ¹/₂ tsp dried) rosemary
500ml/16 fl oz vegetable stock
1-2 tsps lemon juice
1 tsp maple syrup or golden syrup
¹/₄ tsp each salt and white pepper
150g/5¹/₄oz crème fraîche
6 tbsps finely chopped dill

Preparation time: 10 minutes
Cooking time: 20 minutes
Nutritional value:
Analysis per serving, approx:
• 735kJ/175kcal
• 3g protein
• 14g fat
• 8g carbohydrate

Cut a 20cm/8-inch piece off one cucumber and set aside. • Peel the remaining cucumbers thinly, halve lengthways, scrape out the seeds with a teaspoon and cut into 2cm/³/₄-inch cubes. • Boil the diced cucumber with the rosemary and vegetable stock for 20 minutes over a low heat. • Wash reserved cucumber and dry it. Do not peel it but grate it. • When the cucumber is cooked, add the grated cucumber, the lemon juice, maple syrup, salt and pepper to the soup. Fold in the crème fraîche. • Sprinkle with the chopped dill and serve.

Our Tip: The soup can be flavoured with freshly grated horseradish instead of rosemary. For a more substantial dish or as a satisfying evening meal, cook about 400g/14oz floury potatoes with the cucumber. Instead of crème fraîche, mix 100g/4oz crisply-fried diced bacon into the soup. Flavour with borage, thyme or sage instead of dill

Delicious Cauliflower and Courgette-based Soups

Sunflower seeds and meat add nutritional value to these soups

Cauliflower Soup with Sunflower Seeds
In the background

1 cauliflower (about 1kg/2¼lbs)
300g/10oz leeks
1 onion
2 tbsps sunflower oil
1 tbsp wholemeal flour
Pinch of cayenne
1 tsp salt
4 tbsps hulled sunflower seeds
1 tbsp vegetable margarine
4 tbsps young dandelion leaves, chopped (optional)

Preparation time: 30 minutes
Cooking time: 25 minutes
Nutritional value:
Analysis per serving, approx:
• 925kJ/220kcal
• 11g protein
• 11g fat
• 18g carbohydrate

Remove leaves and stalk from the cauliflower and soak in lukewarm water, florets downwards, for 20 minutes to remove any dirt. • Put the cauliflower in a pot, add water to cover and simmer for 25 minutes. • Trim roots and dark green outer leaves from the leeks. Wash the white parts thoroughly and cut into thin rings. Peel and chop the onion finely. • Heat the oil in a large saucepan and sauté the onion until transparent. Add the leek and cook for a further 3 minutes. Sprinkle with flour, and fry briefly. Gradually add 1 l/1¾ pints of the cauliflower cooking water to the onion-and-leek mixture. Bring the soup to the boil several times and season to taste with the cayenne and salt. • Break the cauliflower into florets. Cut the stalk into small pieces, and add these and the florets to the soup and reheat it. • Fry the sunflower seeds in the margarine until golden brown. Sprinkle these and the chopped dandelion leaves over the soup before serving.

Courgette Soup with Breast of Chicken
In the foreground

800g/1¾lbs courgettes
4 shallots • 4 tbsps corn oil
750ml/1¼ pints hot chicken stock
½ tsp salt
1-2 tsps sweet paprika
300g/10oz chicken breast, skinned and boned
4 tbsps single cream
2 tsps sage, finely chopped

Preparation time: 25 minutes
Cooking time: 20 minutes
Nutritional value:
Analysis per serving, approx:
• 1175kJ/280kcal
• 24g protein
• 15g fat
• 13g carbohydrate

Thinly peel and dice two-thirds of the courgettes (about 500g/1lb 2oz). Wash and dry the remaining third. Peel and chop the shallots. • Heat half the oil in a large saucepan. Gently fry the shallots until transparent, add the diced courgettes, cover with the chicken stock and cook, covered, for 15 minutes. • Push the soup through a sieve or blend in a liquidizer and season to taste with the salt and paprika. Cut remaining courgettes, unpeeled, into thin slices, add to the soup and leave to stand for 5 minutes. • Chop the chicken breast. • Heat the remaining oil in a separate pan and fry the chicken for 5 minutes, turning from time to time, then add to the soup. • Stir in the cream and sprinkle with the sage.

Kohlrabi Soup with Meat Dumplings

This makes a one-pot dish for a hearty winter meal

Fennel Soup, Avignon-style

An ideal introduction to fennel

FOR THE SOUP:

1kg/2¼lbs kohlrabi

750ml/1¼ pints vegetable stock

¼ tsp each salt and white pepper

4 tbsps mixed herbs such as lovage and salad burnet

FOR THE DUMPLINGS:

125g/4oz each minced beef and pork

1 egg

5 tbsps breadcrumbs

¼ tsp each salt and white pepper

¼ tsp dried marjoram

Preparation time: 10 minutes
Cooking time: 30 minutes
Nutritional value:
Analysis per serving, approx:
Without the dumplings:
- 400kJ/95kcal
- 6g protein
- 1g fat
- 15g carbohydrate

With the dumplings:
- 1345kJ/320kcal
- 22g protein
- 15g fat
- 24g carbohydrate

Peel the kohlrabi, reserving the green shoots, and cut into julienne strips. • Add these to vegetable stock, bring to the boil and cook, covered, for 20 minutes over a moderate heat. • To make the dumplings combine the minced meat with the egg, breadcrumbs, salt, pepper and marjoram. Knead and shape into walnut-sized dumplings. • Season the soup with the salt and pepper. Add the dumplings to the soup, and simmer, uncovered, over a very low heat for 8-10 minutes. • Add the reserved kohlrabi greens to the herbs. Wash and dry them and chop them finely. • Sprinkle the chopped herbs over the soup before serving.

1kg/2¼lbs fennel

300g/10oz potatoes

1 large onion

3 cloves garlic

1 bay leaf

1 tsp salt

1l/1¾ pints water

2 large cooking apples

1 tbsp butter

3 tbsps chopped parsley

Preparation time: 10 minutes
Cooking time: 25 minutes
Nutritional value:
Analysis per serving, approx:
- 1135kJ/270kcal
- 9g protein
- 3g fat
- 50g carbohydrate

Clean and wash the fennel, reserving the feathery green leaves, then chop finely. Peel and chop the potatoes, onion and garlic. • Bring the prepared vegetables to the boil in the water with the bay leaf and salt, and cook, covered, over a low heat for 25 minutes. • Peel the apples and grate them coarsely. Wash the feathery fennel leaves, dry and chop finely. • Sieve the soup or blend in a liquidizer, and stir in the grated apple. • Heat the butter, and briefly sauté the parsley and fennel greens; sprinkle the soup with the fried herbs before serving.

Our Tip: Leeks may be subistuted for fennel, in which case omit the grated apple. Serve the Leek Soup with croûtons made from white bread, and sprinkle with chopped chives.

Cream of Carrot Soup

In season throughout the year

800g/1 ¾lbs carrots
750ml/1 ¼ pints vegetable stock
1 tbsp flour
3 tbsps butter
½ tsp each salt and white pepper
A few drops lemon juice
Pinch of sugar
2 slices wholemeal bread, cubed
3 tbsps single cream
2 tbsps chopped fresh herbs such as dill, parsley or chives

Preparation time: 15 minutes
Cooking time: 30 minutes
Nutritional value:
Analysis per serving, approx:
- 965kJ/230kcal
- 7g protein
- 10g fat
- 28g carbohydrate

Scrape the carrots, wash thoroughly and dice. Bring to the boil in the vegetable stock, cover and simmer gently over a low heat for 30 minutes.• Blend the carrots and cooking liquid in a liquidizer or food processor, or push through a sieve. Work the flour into 2 tbsps of the butter to form a small ball and use an egg-whisk to beat this into the soup. Cook for a few minutes longer, then season with salt, pepper, lemon juice and sugar.• Fry the bread cubes in the remaining butter until golden.• Add the cream to the soup.• Serve garnished with croûtons and the chopped herbs.

Our Tip: The croûtons in this recipe may be replaced by small balls of sausagemeat. Take 1 or 2 veal or pork sausages and squeeze small balls of meat into the soup. Cook for a few minutes over a low heat.

Minestrone

One of the many versions of this popular soup

Ingredients for 8 servings:

100g/4oz white haricot beans
100g/4oz celery
100g/4oz potatoes
150g/5½oz courgettes
100g/4oz carrots
100g/4oz leeks
100g/4oz peas in the pod
4 tbsps olive oil
1½l/2½ pints chicken stock
1 bay leaf
1 sprig parsley
1 small onion
1 clove garlic
100g/4oz streaky bacon
4 tomatoes
100g/4oz cooked rice
1tsp salt
¼ tsp black pepper
1 tbsp chopped fresh basil
8 tbsps freshly grated Parmesan

Soaking time: 12 hours
Preparation time: 20 minutes
Cooking time: 1½ hours

Nutritional value:

Analysis per serving, approx:
- 1135kJ/270kcal
- 10g protein
- 17g fat
- 19g carbohydrate

Wash the beans in a bowl of cold water, discarding any that float to the surface. • Soak the beans for 12 hours in water that has been boiled, then cooled. • Wash and dry the celery, trim the root end, and slice. Peel, wash and dice the potatoes. Wash and dry the courgettes, and cut into strips. Scrape, wash and dice the carrots. Wash the leeks thoroughly and cut into rings. Shell the peas and add to the other prepared vegetables. • Heat the olive oil in a large saucepan. Sauté all the raw vegetables in the oil for about 3 minutes, then set aside. • Heat the chicken stock with 1½ pints water. Tie the sprig of parsley and bay leaf together. Add the hot chicken stock, the bouquet of herbs and

the beans to the vegetables, and cook covered for a further 30 minutes. • Meanwhile, peel the onion and garlic and chop finely. Dice the bacon and gently fry in a dry frying-pan until the fat runs out. Remove the bacon pieces from the pan and fry the chopped onion and garlic in the bacon fat until golden. • Remove the hard stalk ends from the tomatoes, then skin and chop. • Add the diced tomato, cooked rice, bacon, onion and garlic to the soup. Season to taste with salt and pepper. Serve garnished with the chopped parsley and grated Parmesan.

Our Tip: This is just one authentic Italian recipe for this classic vegetable soup. Ingredients vary according to the region. White or savoy cabbage can be included with the vegetables or tomato purée can be added to the soup. In many areas, taglierini (soup noodles) replace the potato. The basil is often replaced by

other chopped fresh herbs. The Parmesan can either be sprinkled over the soup before serving or handed separately.

Hearty Potato Soups

Take your pick: potato soup with bacon or with watercress

Purée of Potato Soup with Bacon
Illustrated left

400g/14oz floury potatoes
$\frac{1}{2}$ tsp salt
250-500ml/8-16 fl oz meat stock
300g/10oz leeks (white parts only)
$\frac{1}{4}$ tsp salt
100g/4oz streaky bacon
1 large onion
100ml/3 fl oz single cream
2 tbsps chopped parsley

Preparation time: 15 minutes
Cooking time: 20 minutes
Nutritional value:
Analysis per serving, approx:
• 1470kJ/350kcal
• 8g protein
• 25g fat
• 23g carbohydrate

Peel, wash and dice the potatoes. • Cover with water, add salt and bring to the boil. Cook, covered, for 20 minutes. • Heat the meat stock. • Wash the leeks thoroughly, cut them into rings and cook separately, covered, for 15 minutes in a little water. • Dice the bacon. Peel the onion and cut into rings. • Purée the potato together with the water in which it was cooked. Add the leek and its cooking water to the potato purée. Add sufficient meat stock to give a creamy consistency, and stir in the cream. • Fry the bacon in a dry frying-pan until the fat runs. Fry the onion rings in the bacon fat until golden. • Before serving, garnish with the chopped parsley, bacon and onion rings.

Our Tip: Smoked sausage may be substituted for the smoked bacon - garlic sausage is particularly good in this recipe - or Sunday joint leftovers.

Potato Soup with Watercress
Illustrated right

700g/1lb 9oz slightly waxy potatoes
300g/10oz carrots
750ml/1$\frac{1}{4}$ pints vegetable stock
2 shallots
1 clove garlic
300g/10oz watercress or garden cress
2 tbsps safflower oil
1tsp each salt and cayenne

Preparation time: 10 minutes
Cooking time: 15-20 minutes
Nutritional value:
Analysis per serving, approx:
• 985kJ/235kcal
• 7g protein
• 5g fat
• 38g carbohydrate

Peel, wash and dice the potatoes and carrots. • Bring to the boil in the vegetable stock, and cook for 15-20 minutes. • Peel the shallots and garlic and chop finely. Wash the watercress thoroughly, shake dry, and chop roughly. • Heat the oil in a frying-pan and fry the chopped shallots and garlic until golden. Add two-thirds of the watercress, and sauté together for a further 5 minutes. • Add this fried mixture to the soup. Season to taste with salt and cayenne. Before serving, sprinkle with the remaining cress.

Our Tip: Watercress has a milder flavour than garden cress.

White Bean Soup

Makes a fortifying midnight snack!

200g/7oz dried haricot beans
1¹/₂/2 pints boiled water, cooled
1 packet mixed potherbs (parsley, celery, leek, carrot)
1 large potato
1 large onion
1 large carrot
1 green pepper
1 red pepper
¹/₂ tsp each salt and sweet paprika
¹/₄ tsp each white pepper and cayenne
2 beefsteak tomatoes
100g/4oz streaky bacon
2 tbsps chopped parsley

Soaking time: 12 hours
Preparation time: 10 minutes
Cooking time: 1³/₄ hours
Nutritional value:
Analysis per serving, approx:
• 1825kJ/435kcal
• 17g protein
• 18g fat
• 50g carbohydrate

Wash the beans, pick them over, drain, and soak in the boiled water for 12 hours. • Bring the beans to the boil in fresh water, skimming off any scum that rises to the surface. • Trim, wash and roughly chop the potherbs and add to the beans. Cook the beans in a covered saucepan for 1¹/₂ hours. • Peel and dice the potato, onion and carrot. Cut the peppers into strips, discarding the pith and seeds. • Add the chopped vegetables to the cooked beans. Simmer for another 15 minutes, then season to taste with the spices. • Peel and dice the tomatoes, then add to the soup. • Chop the bacon and cook in a dry frying-pan until the fat runs. Add to the soup. • Sprinkle with parsley before serving.

Lentil Soup with Red Wine

A sustaining gourmet dish

300g/10oz lentils
1l/1³/₄ pints water
1 large carrot
1 onion
About ¹/₈ celeriac or 2 sticks celery
2 large potatoes
1 tsp salt
¹/₄ tsp black pepper
125ml/4 fl oz dry red wine
Smoked boiling sausage (optional)

Preparation time: 5 minutes
Cooking time: 1¹/₂ hours
Nutritional value:
Analysis per serving, approx:
• 1535kJ/365kcal
• 21g protein
• 1g fat
• 62g carbohydrate

Wash the lentils in a bowl of water, removing those that float to the top. • Bring to the boil in boiled water, and cook covered for 1-1¹/₂ hours. During the first 15 minutes, repeatedly skim off any scum that forms. • Scrape, wash and dice the carrot. Peel and dice the onion, celeriac or celery and potatoes. • Add the vegetables to the cooked lentils and cook over a low heat for a further 20 minutes. • Season generously with salt and pepper. Remove soup from the heat, and add the red wine.

Our Tip: The lentils may be cooked in a mixture of equal quantities of red wine and water. However, 125ml/4 fl oz red wine should still be added to the finished soup. Lentil Soup is more filling if small rounds of smoked boiling sausage are added shortly before serving.

Leek Soup with Cheese Dumplings

A filling prelude to a refreshing salad

For the soup:

600g/1¼lbs leeks

2 tbsps corn oil

150g/5½oz shelled peas

1 l/1¾ pints vegetable stock

Pinch each of nutmeg, salt and white pepper

For the cheese dumplings:

50g/2oz vegetable margarine, softened

1 egg

50g/2oz wholewheat semolina

40g/1½oz freshly grated Cheddar cheese

¼tsp each grated lemon rind, salt and white pepper

To garnish:

2 tbsps chopped chives

Preparation time: 40 minutes
Cooking time: 20 minutes
Nutritional value:
Analysis per serving, approx:
- 1260kJ/300kcal
- 13g protein
- 16g fat
- 25g carbohydrate

Trim the coarse green leaves and roots from the leeks. Slit lengthways, wash thoroughly and slice thinly.• Heat the oil in a large saucepan. Sauté the leek in the oil, add the peas and the vegetable stock. Cook, covered, for 20 minutes.• To make the dumplings, beat the margarine and egg together and gradually incorporate the semolina, grated cheese and seasoning. Let the dough stand for 20 minutes.• Bring some salted water to the boil in another saucepan. Using a moistened teaspoon, scoop out balls of dough and add to the boiling water. Leave to cook for 10-15 minutes.• Season the soup to taste with nutmeg, salt and pepper. Add the cheese dumplings to the soup. Before serving, sprinkle with the chopped chives.

Waldorf Salad

A classic starter or part of an elegant cold buffet

300g/10oz celeriac or 1 head celery

200g/7oz tart eating apples (such as Granny Smiths)

2 tbsps lemon juice

$^1/_2$ tsp salt

50g/2oz shelled walnuts

150g/5$^1/_2$oz mayonnaise

125ml/4 fl oz single cream

$^1/_2$-1 tsp sugar

Preparation time: 15 minutes
Standing time: 1 hour
Nutritional value:
Analysis per serving, approx:
• 1825kJ/435kcal
• 5g protein
• 38g fat
• 18g carbohydrate

Peel, wash and dry the celeriac or celery. Cut celeriac into julienne strips or chop the celery. Peel the apple, remove the core and cut it into julienne strips. Carefully combine the celeriac or celery and apple and sprinkle the lemon juice over them to prevent discolouration. Sprinkle with the salt, cover, and refrigerate for 1 hour to allow the flavours to blend.• Chop the walnuts and combine with the mayonnaise, cream and sugar. Fold the walnut-flavoured mayonnaise into the salad before serving.• Crisp, freshly baked French bread is delicious with this salad

Grilled Aubergines

This recipe greatly enhances the distinctive flavour of the vegetable

2 medium-sized aubergines (500g/1lb 2oz)
1 tbsp lemon juice
3 cloves garlic
2 tbsps bottled green peppercorns
6 tbsps olive oil
2 tbsps fresh thyme
1 tsp salt
1/4 tsp black pepper

Preparation time including standing time: 1 hour 40 minutes
Cooking time: 25 minutes
Nutritional value:
Analysis per serving, approx:
- 860kJ/205kcal
- 4g protein
- 16g fat
- 11g carbohydrate

Wash and dry the aubergines. Remove the stalk ends and halve lengthways. Rub the cut surfaces with the lemon juice. Peel the garlic and chop it finely. Chop the green peppercorns coarsely.

Mix the chopped garlic, green peppercorns, thyme, salt and black pepper into the olive oil. Place each halved aubergine, cut side uppermost, on a large piece of aluminium foil. Prick the cut surfaces deeply with a fork, and pour liberal amounts of the flavoured oil over them. Wrap the aubergines in the foil, and leave to stand for 1½ hours in the refrigerator. • Preheat the oven to 230°C/450°F/Gas Mark 8 or preheat the grill. • Place the aubergines, wrapped in foil, on the rack of the oven or grill, cut side down, and grill for 10 minutes. Then open the foil packages, and, with the cut surface facing up, cook directly under the grill or on the top shelf of the oven for another 15 minutes. • If desired, the aubergines can be served on their foil wrapping with the rest of the seasoned olive oil poured over them.

Baked Tomatoes with Mozzarella

A delicious and attractive starter, hot or cold

4 large beefsteak tomatoes (800g/1³/₄lbs)
300g/10oz mozzarella cheese
2 medium-sized onions
2 cloves garlic
1/2 tsp salt
1/4 tsp white pepper
2 tbsps olive oil
1/4-1/2 tsp fresh thyme leaves
Olive oil for greasing

Preparation time: 10 minutes
Cooking time: 25 minutes
Nutritional value:
Analysis per serving, approx:
- 1700kJ/405kcal
- 22g protein
- 30g fat
- 11g carbohydrate

Lightly grease a shallow ovenproof dish with a little oil. • Preheat the oven to 220°C/430°F/Gas Mark 7. • Wash and dry the tomatoes, and cut them and the cheese into slices about 1 cm/¹/₂ inch thick. Arrange slices of cheese and tomato in alternating, overlapping layers in the ovenproof dish. Peel the onions and garlic, and chop finely. Sprinkle the salt over the chopped garlic and mash together with a fork. Mix the chopped onion, garlic and pepper with the olive oil, and trickle this over the sliced tomato and mozzarella. • Bake on the middle shelf of the preheated oven for 20 minutes. • Wash and dry the thyme and sprinkle it over the dish. Cook for a further 5 minutes. • Freshly baked French bread is good with this dish.

Our Tip: To serve Tomatoes with Mozzarella as a cold starter, season with chopped basil instead of thyme.

Grilled Avocados

A choice starter for an elegant supper

2 avocados (about 400g/14oz)
2 tsps lemon juice
12 anchovy fillets
2 tbsps small capers
1/2 onion
Dash of Tabasco sauce
1 tbsp walnut oil
4 tbsps crème fraîche
2 slices Cheddar cheese

Preparation time: 10 minutes
Cooking time: 10-15 minutes
Nutritional value:
Analysis per serving, approx:
• 1365kJ/325kcal
• 7g protein
• 30g fat
• 6g carbohydrate

Preheat the oven to 230°C/450°F/Gas Mark 8, or turn on the electric grill. • Wash, dry and halve the avocados and remove the stones. Remove two-thirds of the flesh, chop finely, and drizzle lemon juice over both the flesh remaining in the skins and the chopped avocado. • Cut a sliver off the rounded bottom of the halved avocados so that they sit firmly. Chop the anchovies, capers and peeled half-onion finely, and combine with the chopped avocado, Tabasco sauce, oil and crème fraîche. Stuff the avocados with the creamy mixture, and place on the a baking dish in the oven or under the grill. Dice the slices of cheese and scatter over the avocados. • Bake or grill until the cheese has melted and a golden-brown crust has formed.

Our Tip: For the filling, 2 chopped herring fillets and a gherkin may be substituted for the anchovies and capers.

Fennel with Aïoli

Typically Mediterranean

4 medium-sized fennel bulbs (about 800g/1³/₄lbs)
2 tsps lemon juice
1 egg-sized piece of white crustless bread
1/2 cup milk
6 cloves garlic
2 egg yolks
250ml/8fl oz cold-pressed olive oil
1-2 tsps tarragon vinegar
1/2 tsp salt
Pinch of white pepper

Preparation time: 20 minutes
Nutritional value:
Analysis per serving, approx:
• About 3130kJ/745kcal
• 8g protein
• 67g fat
• 27g carbohydrate

Remove the feathery green leaves from the fennel bulbs, wash and pat dry. Chop finely, cover, and set aside. • Discard the outer tough ribs of the fennel bulbs. Shred the fennel, sprinkle with the lemon juice, cover and set aside. • Soak the bread in the cold milk. Peel the garlic and crush through a garlic press into a bowl. Squeeze any excess moisture from the moistened bread, add it and the egg yolks to the crushed garlic, and mix well. Then add the olive oil into the garlic mixture, a drop at a time to start with, then a teaspoonful at a time until you have a sauce with the consistency of mayonnaise. Flavour to taste with the tarragon vinegar, salt and pepper. Serve the aïoli in a small bowl sprinkled with the chopped fennel green. • Place the bowl on a tray with the fennel arranged around it. The strips of fennel are eaten with the aïoli sauce. • Fresh French bread and dry white wine are good accompaniments.

Tomatoes Stuffed with Tuna and Rice

An entrée or a light supper

8 medium-sized tomatoes
1 tsp salt
150g/5½oz long-grain rice, cooked
200g/7oz canned tuna
2 tbsps chopped parsley
¼ tsp black pepper
½ tsp grated lemon rind
4 tbsps crème fraîche
8 small basil leaves

Preparation time: 10 minutes
Nutritional value:
Analysis per serving, approx:
- 1135kJ/270kcal
- 17g protein
- 15g fat
- 17g carbohydrate

Wash and dry the tomatoes and, using a sharp knife, cut a small slice from the bottom of each tomato to make a 'lid'. Use a pointed teaspoon to scoop out the flesh and seeds and sprinkle with salt.• Place the rice in a bowl. Drain the tuna, break into small pieces and add it with the chopped parsley, pepper, lemon rind and crème fraîche to the rice. Fold in lightly.• Fill the tomatoes with the tuna and rice stuffing, placing the 'lids' on top.• Wash the basil leaves, pat dry, and use to garnish the tomatoes.

Our Tip: When using grated lemon rind or unpeeled wedges of lemon, always buy untreated fruit. Instead of tuna, bean sprouts may be used, in which case omit the lemon rind. The scooped-out flesh of the tomatoes may be used to make an Italian pasta sauce: sauté 1 finely chopped onion and 1 clove garlic in 1 tbsp olive oil, add the tomatoes and cook until reduced to a thickish consistency. Season with dried oregano, salt and freshly ground black pepper.

Swiss Chard au Gratin

Swiss Chard can also be used wherever spinach is called for

500g/1lb 2oz young Swiss chard
500ml/16 fl oz water
¹/₂ tsp salt
4 slices white bread, crusts removed
4 tbsps butter
2 eggs
4 tbsps crème fraîche
¹/₄ tsp salt
50g/2oz freshly grated Cheddar cheese

Preparation time: 10 minutes
Cooking time: 15 minutes
Nutritional value:
Analysis per serving, approx:
• 1050kJ/250kcal
• 13g protein
• 16g fat
· 14g carbohydrate

Remove the coarse stems and ribs from the Swiss chard, wash it and leave to drain. • Bring the salted water to the boil, add the Swiss chard leaves. Cover and cook over a low heat for 5 minutes. • Drain in a colander, then shred. • Preheat the oven to 220°C/430°F/Gas Mark 7. • Lightly toast the slices of bread and spread thinly with 15g/¹/₂ oz of the butter. • Beat the eggs, crème fraîche and salt together. Heat the remaining butter in a frying pan, and cook the egg mixture until barely set, stirring constantly. • Divide the Swiss chard among the pieces of toast, and place the lightly set egg on top. Sprinkle each with grated cheese. • Place on a baking sheet on the top shelf of the oven and bake for 10 minutes or until the cheese has formed a golden crust.

Our Tip: Young spinach leaves may be substituted for Swiss chard. Blanch spinach for 1 minute in 1 l/1¹/₂ pints of boiling water. Drain well before placing on the buttered toast.

Asparagus Tips au Gratin

An epicurean treat for asparagus lovers

1kg/2¹/₄lbs asparagus
1tsp salt
1 sugar cube
4 slices white bread, each weighing 50g/2oz
2 tbsps soft butter
200g/7oz cooked prawns
4 tbsps crème fraîche
4 tbsps freshly grated Jarlsberg cheese
2 tbsps finely chopped dill

Preparation time: 15 minutes
Cooking time: 30 minutes
Nutritional value:
Analysis per serving, approx:
• 1490kJ/355kcal
• 23g protein
• 13g fat
• 37g carbohydrate

Preheat the oven to 220°C/ 430°F/Gas Mark 7. If using white asparagus, thinly peel it from top to bottom, and cut off the woody ends. • Bring the salt and sugar to the boil in 2 l/3¹/₂ pints of water. Tie the asparagus spears into three bundles, and cook in a covered saucepan for 10-15 minutes depending on thickness of stems. • Drain the asparagus and cut about 6cm/2¹/₂in off the tips (Reserve the rest of the stems and the cooking water to make soup.) • Spread the bread with butter. • Rinse the prawns in cold water and drain. Divide the asparagus tips between the slices of bread and arrange the prawns on top. • Place the slices of bread on a baking sheet lined with aluminium foil. Combine the crème fraîche and the grated cheese, and pour this over the prawns. • Cook on the middle shelf of the oven until the top is golden brown. • Garnish with dill. • A green salad is a good accompaniment.

Our Tip: Salsify may be prepared in the same way

Spinach Soufflés

A popular light starter

1kg/2¼lbs fresh spinach
1 l/1¾ pints water
1 tsp salt
6 shallots
Small bunch parsley, chopped
2 tbsps oil
2 tsps lemon juice
125ml/4 fl oz milk
3 tbsps butter
4 tbsps flour
¼ tsp cayenne
Pinch of grated nutmeg
50g/2oz grated Parmesan
4 eggs
½ tsp salt
¼ tsp black pepper
Butter to grease the soufflé dishes

Preparation time: 1 hour
Cooking time: 25 minutes
Nutritional value:
Analysis per serving, approx:
• 1615kJ/385kcal
• 22g protein
• 23g fat
• 22g carbohydrate

Pick over the spinach, wash and blanch for 1 minute in boiling salted water. Drain. Chop the parsley • Peel the shallots, chop finely and sauté in the oil. Add the spinach, parsley and lemon juice, mix well, and remove from the heat.• Preheat oven to 180°C/ 350°F/Gas Mark 4.• Heat the milk. Make a white sauce using the butter, flour and milk, and bring to the boil, stirring all the time. Season to taste with the cayenne and nutmeg, remove from heat and stir in the cheese. Separate the eggs. Incorporate the egg yolks one by one into the béchamel sauce. Stir in the spinach and season with salt and pepper.• Butter four ramekin dishes.• Beat the egg whites until they are stiff, and fold into the spinach mixture.• Divide between the ramekins, which should be no more than two-thirds full, and bake for 25 minutes on the middle shelf of the oven.• Serve immediately.

Broccoli Soufflé

Soufflés should be served straight from the oven

800g/1¾lbs broccoli
2l/3½ pints water
1 tsp salt
2 tbsps cornflour
4 tbsps crème fraîche
3 eggs
¼ tsp salt
50g/2oz freshly-grated Parmesan
Butter to grease the dish

Preparation time: 45 minutes
Cooking time: 40 minutes
Nutritional value:
Analysis per serving, approx:
• 985kJ/235kcal
• 19g protein
• 12g fat
• 13g carbohydrate

Clean the broccoli, separate the florets from the stems, and chop the stems roughly. Cook the broccoli in boiling salted water for 10 minutes.• Preheat the oven to 200°C/400°F/Gas Mark 6.• Combine the cornflour and crème fraîche.• Purée the broccoli in batches in a liquidizer or food processor, adding a couple of tablespoons of cooking water to each batch. Mix the purée with the crème fraîche and bring the whole mixture to the boil, stirring constantly.• Separate the eggs. Mix the yolks and the salt into the slightly cooled broccoli purée.• Beat the egg whites until stiff, and fold, together with the Parmesan cheese, into the broccoli purée.• Butter a soufflé dish large enough for the mixture to come just two-thirds of the way up the side. Pour the broccoli mixture into the dish, and cook on the middle shelf of the oven for 40 minutes.• Serve the soufflé immediately.• Wild rice or brown rice with a little melted butter make good accompaniments to this rich soufflé.

Pickled French Beans

A useful standby for unexpected guests

For 8 servings

2kg/4¹/₂lbs French beans
4l/5 pints water
1 tbsp salt
1 bunch savory
750g/1 lb 10oz sugar
3 cloves
2 tsps turmeric
750ml/1¹/₄ pints white wine vinegar

Preparation time: 1 hour
Cooking time: 20 minutes
Standing time: 3 days
Nutritional value:

Analysis per serving, approx:
• 2060kJ/490kcal
• 5g protein
• 0g fat
• 109g carbohydrate

Top, tail and wash the beans.•
Bring the water to the boil with salt and savory. Cook the beans, covered, in this liquid for 15 minutes.• Drain the beans in a colander, reserving the water. Remove the savory.• Put 250ml/8 fl oz of the cooking water in a saucepan. Add the sugar, cloves and turmeric, and bring to the boil, stirring constantly until the sugar has dissolved. Add the vinegar and boil for another 5 minutes, uncovered.• Put the beans into a large bottling jar. Pour the hot pickling liquid over the beans, seal the jar and leave to cool.• Refrigerate the pickled beans. Once a day, for three days, drain the beans over a saucepan. Bring the liquid to the boil, return beans to the jar, and pour the hot liquid over them. • The beans keep well in the refrigerator for up to four weeks.• Serve with fresh French or garlic bread

Hungarian-style Peppers

A spicy snack

For 8 servings

3 yellow peppers
3 red peppers
3 green peppers
500g/1lb 2oz shallots
2 cloves garlic
2 tsps salt
1 tsp dried oregano
750ml/1¹/₄ pints fruit vinegar
2 bay leaves
600g/1lb 6oz sugar

Preparation time: 40 minutes
Cooking time: 10 minutes
Standing time: 3 days
Nutritional value:

Analysis per serving, approx:
• 1680kJ/400kcal
• 4g protein
• 0g fat
• 90g carbohydrate

Preheat the oven to 250°C/
480°F/Gas Mark 8.• Place the peppers on a baking sheet on the middle shelf of the oven and bake until the thin outer skin splits. Then cool the peppers and peel off the skin.• Peel and quarter the shallots. Peel the garlic and mash with the salt. Cut the peppers in four, discard the pith and seeds, and cut into pieces; place in a saucepan with the shallots, garlic purée, oregano, vinegar, bay leaves and sugar. Add sufficient water to cover completely.• Boil for 10 minutes, cool slightly, then tip into a crock with the brine. Leave to cool completely, and store, covered, in the refrigerator.• Every day for the next three days, drain the pickling liquid from the peppers, bring it to the boil, and pour it back over the vegetables while still hot.• The peppers can then be stored in a tightly-closed jar in the refrigerator for up to 4 weeks.• Farmhouse bread and cold poultry are good accompaniments for Hungarian-style Peppers.

Sweet-and-sour Mixed Vegetables

Okra adds an exotic touch

For 8 servings
1kg/2¼lbs ripe tomatoes
500g/1lb 2oz shallots
500g/1lb 2oz okra
Juice and grated rind of 1 lemon
1 tbsp salt
4 white peppercorns
10 mustard seeds
750g/1¾lbs sugar
750ml/1¼ pints cider vinegar

Preparation time: 30 minutes
Standing time: 3 days
Nutritional value:
Analysis per serving, approx:
• 1975kJ/470kcal
• 4g protein
• 0g fat
• 109g carbohydrate per serving

Pour boiling water over the tomatoes, skin and halve them, removing the hard stalk ends. Peel and halve the shallots. Wash, top and tail the okra, and slit them in half lengthways. • Put the lemon juice, lemon rind, salt, peppercorns, mustard seeds, sugar and vinegar in a saucepan and bring to the boil, stirring constantly until the sugar has completely dissolved. Pour this liquid over the prepared, mixed vegetables. Cover, and leave to stand for 12 hours. • Drain the vegetables in a colander, catching the liquid in a saucepan. Return to the boil and cook for 5 minutes, then pour it over the vegetables again while still hot. When cool, cover and refrigerate. • Once a day, for the next two days, drain the vegetables over a saucepan, bring the liquid to the boil, return the vegetables to the crock and pour the reheated liquid over them. • The vegetables taste best if stored in the refrigerator for about 4 weeks. • Remove the vegetables from the refrigerator at least an hour before serving. • Fresh rye bread and salami are good accompaniments.

Vegetables as a Main Course

Classic vegetable dishes alternate with unusual creations. Some new discoveries will soon become favourites

Creamed Sorrel with Poached Eggs

A fresh and mild flavour

2 spring onions
80g/3oz young sorrel leaves
300g/10oz cucumber
1 tbsp vegetable margarine
Pinch of salt
1 tsp honey
1 tsp mild mustard
Pinch of white pepper
1 small pot thick-set natural yogurt
125ml/4fl oz whipping cream
2 tbsps chopped dill
2l/3½ pints water • 1 tsp salt
2 tbsps vinegar
4 eggs
4 slices wholemeal bread

Preparation time: 30 minutes
Nutritional value:

Analysis per serving, approx:
• 945kJ/225kcal
• 5g protein
• 15g fat
• 17g carbohydrate

Trim and wash the spring onions and chop finely. Pick over the sorrel, removing any coarse stems, wash, shake dry and chop. Wash, dry and skin the cucumber, then grate. • Melt the margarine, and fry the spring onion until transparent. Add the sorrel, and cook gently for 5 minutes. Allow the vegetables to cool, and mix with the cucumber, salt, honey, mustard and pepper. Stir in the yogurt. Beat the cream until it thickens, fold into the other ingredients, and sprinkle with dill. Bring the water to the boil with the salt and vinegar. Break the eggs one at a time into a cup, and gently lower into the boiling water. Let the water come back to the boil, remove the saucepan from the heat immediately and leave the eggs to stand in the hot water for 5 minutes. Toast the bread. Use a slotted spoon to lift the eggs out of the water, and serve on the toast. • Serve the creamed sorrel separately.

Wild Herb Omelette

Use a mixture of wild spring greens

150g/5½oz mixed wild herbs (hogweed, comfrey, great plantain, ox-eye daisies, shepherd's purse, chervil, nettles, dandelions, etc.)
2 shallots
1 clove garlic
½ tsp salt
3 tbsps corn oil
A pinch of salt and white pepper
8 eggs
5 tbsps single cream
½ tsp salt
¼ tsp black pepper

Preparation time: 40 minutes
Nutritional value:

Analysis per serving, approx:
• 1260kJ/300kcal
• 17g protein
• 23g fat
• 7g carbohydrate

Pick over the herbs, removing any thick stems. Wash them thoroughly, shake dry and chop.

Peel and chop the shallots and garlic and add the salt. • Fry the shallots in 1 tbsp oil until transparent. Add the herbs and garlic, and cook gently for 5 minutes, stirring occasionally. Season with salt and pepper. • Beat the eggs with the cream, salt and pepper. Heat a quarter of the remaining oil in a frying-pan, add a quarter of the egg mixture. Move around with the back of the spoon for the first few minutes, then tipping the pan slightly in different directions until the mixture starts to set, but the surface is still runny. Put a quarter of the herb mixture on one half of the omelette. Fold the omelette over, and slide it onto a preheated serving dish. Repeat until all four omelettes are ready. Keep the omelettes warm in the oven at lowest setting until ready to serve. • Mushrooms fried in butter and new potatoes make good accompaniments.

Making a Meal of Asparagus

The asparagus season is short – make the most of it!

Asparagus, Classic-style

Illustrated in background

1½kg/3lbs 6oz very fresh asparagus spears
1 tsp salt
1 sugar lump
200g/7oz butter

Preparation time: 15 minutes
Cooking time: 15-20 minutes
Nutritional value:
Analysis per serving, approx:
• 1975kJ/470kcal
• 8g protein
• 42g fat
• 15g carbohydrate

Peel a thin layer off each stem of asparagus with an asparagus peeler or a knife, starting below the head and working from top to bottom; cut off the woody ends. Rinse the asparagus in cold water. Use kitchen string to tie the asparagus into bundles of 6-10 stems. • Using a large saucepan or asparagus cooker, bring enough water to the boil to cover the bundles of asparagus, then add the salt and sugar. Place the bundles in the boiling water, and cook, covered, for 15-20 minutes. The asparagus tips should not disintegrate or become too soft. Have another large pan of boiling water ready. • Melt the butter, pour it into a sauceboat and stand over a bain-marie or double boiler. • Lift the cooked asparagus out of the water and plunge briefly into the second pan of boiling salted water, Then drain the bundles on a thick layer of tea-towels, and serve on a heated plate, or a special asparagus dish with a perforated surface that allows the liquid to drain off. Discard the string before serving

Baked Asparagus au Gratin

Illustrated in foreground

1½kg/3lbs 6oz very fresh asparagus spears
1 tsp salt • 1 sugar lump
1 onion • 25g/1oz butter
3 tbsps flour
125ml/4fl oz hot veal stock
125ml/4fl oz warm milk
Pinch of salt
Pinch each of grated nutmeg, white pepper and dried thyme
50g/2oz grated Cheddar cheese
2 egg yolks
4 tbsps single cream

Preparation time: 20 minutes
Cooking time: 25-35 minutes
Nutritional value:
Analysis per serving, approx:
• 1300kJ/310kcal
• 18g protein
• 16g fat
• 24g carbohydrate

Prepare and cook the asparagus as for the previous recipe. Peel and dice the onion. Heat the butter and fry the diced onion in it until it is transparent. Sprinkle the flour over it and allow it to cook a little, stirring constantly. Gradually add the veal stock, letting the mixture reach boiling point each time some stock is added. Stir in the warm milk, and bring the sauce to the boil again. Season to taste with the salt, nutmeg, pepper and crushed thyme. Stir the grated cheese into the sauce. Beat the egg yolks and the cream together. Stir 4 tbsps of the hot sauce into the egg mixture. Remove the sauce from the heat and fold in the egg and cream mixture. • Preheat the oven to 230°C/450°F/Gas Mark 8. • Drain the asparagus well and arrange it in an ovenproof dish. Pour the sauce over it. Cook on the middle shelf of the oven for 10-15 minutes.

Potato Croquettes

Simple but always tasty

800g/1³/₄lbs floury potatoes
50g/2oz streaky bacon
2 large onions
100g/4oz cracked wheat, finely crushed
2 eggs
1 tsp salt
¹/₄ tsp white pepper
¹/₂ tsp dried or 2 tsps marjoram, freshly chopped
5 tbsps breadcrumbs
3 tbsps oil

Preparation time: 20 minutes
Cooking time: 40-45 minutes
Nutritional value:
Analysis per serving, approx:
• 2060kJ/490kcal
• 15g protein
• 20g fat
• 62g carbohydrate

Scrub the potatoes under running water, then boil, covered, in water for 30-35 minutes or until really soft. • Drain and cool. • Dice the bacon. Peel the onions and chop finely. • Peel the potatoes and mash until smooth. Fry the bacon in a dry frying-pan until the fat runs; remove it and fry the onions in the fat until transparent. Add to the puréed potato. Add the cracked wheat, eggs, salt, pepper and marjoram, and work into a smooth, but dry paste. • Shape into croquettes about 5cm/2 inches across and 2cm/³/₄ inch thick. Coat in breadcrumbs and fry in the hot oil until brown and crisp all over. • Serve with a mixed green salad.

Our Tip: For less fattening croquettes, use finely diced, lean ham instead of bacon and omit the breadcrumbs.

Potato Pancakes on Spinach

Potato pancakes with a difference

400g/14oz floury potatoes
3 tbsps flour
1 tsp salt
500g/1lb 2oz spinach
¹/₂ tsp salt
Pinch of grated nutmeg
50g/20z melted butter
4 rashers streaky bacon
4 eggs
¹/₄ tsp each salt and coarsely ground black pepper

Preparation time: 30 minutes
Cooking time: 20 minutes
Nutritional value:
Analysis per serving, approx:
• 1535kJ/365kcal
• 13g protein
• 23g fat
• 24g carbohydrate

Wash, peel and grate the potatoes and mix with the flour and salt. Cover and set aside. • Pick over the spinach, wash and cook, covered, over a low heat for 10 minutes or until it wilts. Season with salt and nutmeg, and keep warm in a cool oven. Divide potato mixture into 4 equal-sized patties. Melt the butter and fry the potato patties in it. Keep warm. • Fry the bacon rashers in the same pan until crisp. Remove and keep warm • Fry the eggs in the remaining fat. Sprinkle salt over the egg whites, and coarsely milled pepper over the yolks. • Divide the spinach between four individual plates. Top with a potato pancake, an egg and a rasher of bacon.

Potatoes in Béchamel Sauce with Peas

Best made with new potatoes

1kg/2 ¼lbs firm potatoes
600g/1lb 6oz peas in the pod
125ml/4 fl oz water
Pinch of salt
Large bunch of mixed herbs (dill, chervil, lovage, parsley,tarragon, chives, etc.)
1 onion
25g/1oz butter
1 tbsp flour
125ml/4fl oz warm milk
¼ tsp each salt and white pepper
4 tbsps single cream

Preparation time: 15 minutes
Cooking time: 30-35 minutes
Nutritional value:
Analysis per serving, approx:
- 1700kJ/405kcal
- 19g protein
- 9g fat
- 62g carbohydrate

Scrub the potatoes under running water and boil, barely covered with water, for 30-35 minutes. Drain, skin and slice. • Shell the peas and boil in salted water for 6-9 minutes depending on their size. Drain them, reserving the cooking liquid. Cover and set aside. • Wash the herbs, shake them dry and chop them. Peel and chop the onion. • Heat the butter and fry the onion until transparent. Sprinkle with flour and cook until it begins to change colour, stirring constantly. Gradually add the pea cooking water. Stir in the milk. Let the sauce simmer for a few minutes, then season to taste with salt and pepper. • Reheat the sliced potato and the peas in the sauce. Finally, stir in the cream and sprinkle with herbs.

Our Tip: French beans may be substituted for the peas, or garnish with diced green pepper. To make this a meat meal, mix diced bacon or sliced smoked sausage into the sauce.

Stuffed Peppers

Many types of stuffing may be used for peppers

Green Peppers with Minced Meat
Illustrated in foreground

4 large green peppers
Salt • 1 large onion
2 cloves garlic
100g/4oz button mushrooms
2 tbsps oil
200g/7 oz each minced pork and beef
200g/7oz long-grain rice, cooked
1 egg • 1/2 tsp dried rosemary
2 tbsps chopped parsley
250ml/8 fl oz beef stock
4 tbsps tomato purée
100ml/3 fl oz natural yogurt
Pinch each of sugar, salt and sweet paprika

Preparation time: 20 minutes
Cooking time: 40 minutes
Nutritional value:
Analysis per serving, approx:
• 2165 kJ/515kcal
• 28g protein
• 31g fat
• 31g carbohydrate

Slice a 'lid' from the stem end of the peppers. Discard the seeds and pith, wash and sprinkle the peppers inside with salt. Peel the onion and garlic and chop finely. Wash and trim the mushrooms and slice thinly. • Heat the oil. Fry the onion and garlic until transparent. Add the mushrooms and meat and fry together briefly, turning occasionally. • Add the rice, 1 tsp salt, egg, rosemary and parsley to the mince. Fill the peppers with this mixture. • Place the stuffed peppers in a saucepan with a tight-fitting lid, pour the beef stock over them, and stew for 40 minutes over gentle heat. • Remove the peppers to a dish and keep warm. Mix the cooking liquid with the tomato purée and the yogurt, reheat and season with the sugar, salt and paprika. Serve sauce separately.

Red Peppers with Cracked Wheat
Illustrated in background

4 large red peppers
1 large onion
4 small tomatoes
1 tbsp corn oil
8 tbsps cracked wheat, soaked in water for 15 minutes
2 eggs
4 tbsps chopped mixed herbs
1 tsp salt • 1/4 tsp cayenne
250ml/8fl oz hot vegetable stock
2 tbsps crème fraîche
4 tbsps grated Jarlsberg cheese
2 tbsps shelled sunflower seeds, chopped • 1 tsp arrowroot
4 tbsps orange juice

Preparation time: 20 minutes
Cooking time: 40 minutes
Nutritional value:
Analysis per serving, approx:
• 1300kJ/310kcal
• 15g protein
• 14g fat
• 31g carbohydrate

Remove tops from peppers to make lids. Remove the seeds and pith. Peel the onion, and chop finely. Skin and dice the tomatoes. • Gently sauté the chopped onion in the oil until transparent. Drain the cracked wheat, add it to the pan and fry briefly. Remove from the heat and mix with the tomatoes, eggs, herbs and seasoning. Fill the peppers with this mixture, place in a saucepan and pour the stock round them. Combine the crème fraîche, cheese and sunflower seeds and spread over the stuffing. Lastly top with the reserved 'lids'. Cover the pan and braise the stuffed peppers over a low heat for about 40 minutes. Remove peppers to a serving dish and keep warm. • Stir the arrowroot into the orange juice and use this to thicken the cooking liquid. Season with salt and cayenne.

Stuffed Potatoes

These potatoes make a nutritious and economical meal

250g/8oz button mushrooms
1 large onion
2 tbsps corn oil
1 tbsp chopped parsley
Salt and white pepper
1 small egg
2 tbsps fresh breadcrumbs
8 medium floury potatoes (1kg/2¼lbs)
500ml/16 fl oz vegetable stock
1 tbsp wholewheat flour
125ml/4 fl oz natural yogurt

Preparation time: 35 minutes
Cooking time: 35 minutes
Nutritional value:
Analysis per serving, approx:
- 1450kJ/345kcal
- 12g protein
- 10g fat
- 51g carbohydrate per serving

Trim, wash and chop the mushrooms. Peel and chop the onion finely and fry in 1 tbsp hot oil until transparent. Add mushrooms and parsley, and cook gently for 5 minutes in a covered pan. Remove vegetables from the heat and season with salt and pepper; leave to cool slightly. Add the egg and sufficient breadcrumbs to produce a smooth, firm consistency. • Peel the potatoes, wash, dry, and cut off the top third lengthways to make a lid. Scoop out the potatoes, being careful not to damage the skins, and stuff with the vegetable mixture. Replace the lid and tie with kitchen string. Fry the potatoes all over in the rest of the oil. Heat the vegetable stock, add it to the potatoes, and braise in a covered saucepan over a low heat for 35 minutes. • Remove the potatoes from the stock and keep warm. Mix the flour with a little cold water, beating well until no lumps remain. Gradually add to the stock, return to the boil and cook for a few minutes, stirring. Add the yogurt to this sauce and season with salt and pepper.

Stuffed Aubergines

A sustaining meal

2 medium-sized aubergines (600g/1lb 6oz) • ½ tsp salt
100g/4oz streaky bacon
2 onions • 1 clove garlic
4 tomatoes
200g/7oz button mushrooms
300g/10oz long-grain rice, cooked
½ tsp each salt and sweet paprika
¼ tsp each pepper and ground caraway seeds
1 tbsp chopped parsley
4 tbsps grated Cheddar cheese
375ml/15 fl oz vegetable stock
100ml/4 fl oz natural yogurt
2 tsps cornflour
3 tbsps tomato purée
Pinch of sugar

Preparation time: 30 minutes
Cooking time: 40 minutes
Nutritional value:
Analysis per serving, approx:
- 1680kJ/400kcal
- 13g protein
- 23g fat • 35g carbohydrate

Halve the aubergines lengthways. Scoop out the flesh, and chop finely. Salt the insides of the aubergines. Dice the bacon. Peel the onions and garlic, and chop finely. Skin the tomatoes and chop finely. Trim the mushrooms, and slice thinly. • Preheat the oven to 200°C/ 400°F/Gas Mark 6. • Fry the bacon in a dry frying-pan until the fat runs. Add the onions, garlic, mushrooms and chopped aubergine and sauté together, stirring occasionally. Add the tomatoes, and cook, covered, for 5 minutes. Mix in the rice; season with the spices and parsley. Stuff the aubergines and sprinkle with cheese: put in a baking dish, pour hot vegetable stock round the aubergines and bake in the oven for 40 minutes. • Soften the cornflour in a little cold water and combine with the cooking liquid, yogurt, tomato purée and sugar in a saucepan. Bring briefly to the boil. Serve the sauce separately.

Carrots in a New Light

Tasty carrot recipes

Carrots with Mango and Fillet of Pork

Illustrated on the right

600g/1lb 6oz lean pork fillet

2 onions

750g/1lb 10oz carrots

1 large ripe mango

50g/2oz raisins

3 tbsps orange juice, freshly squeezed if possible

500ml/16 fl oz beef stock

3 tbsps sunflower oil

1 tbsp flour

1/4 tsp each salt, cayenne and sugar

Preparation time: 30 minutes
Cooking time: 25 minutes
Nutritional value:
Analysis per serving, approx:
• 2140kJ/510kcal
• 32g protein
• 24g fat
• 41g carbohydrate

Wash, dry and cube the meat. Peel and chop the onions. Scrape, wash and slice the carrots. Halve the mango, remove the stone, peel and chop the fruit. Wash the raisins in hot water, drain, and soak in the orange juice. Heat the beef stock. • Heat the oil. Fry the chopped onion until transparent, add the meat and brown lightly. Add the carrots to the meat and sprinkle with the flour. Cook for a few minutes, then gradually stir in the hot stock. Cover and braise for 20 minutes. • Season to taste with the salt, cayenne and sugar. Add the diced mango, raisins and orange juice, and cook for a further 5 minutes to allow the flavours to combine.

Our Tip: Serve with Parisian Potatoes.
Use a melon scoop to make small potato balls. Boil in salted water and toss in melted butter.

Carrot Medley with Whipped Cream

Illustrated on the left

800g/1³/₄lbs carrots

3 spring onions

500g/1lb 2oz floury potatoes

3 tbsps vegetable margarine

2 tbsps maple or golden syrup

200ml/7 fl oz hot vegetable stock

125ml/4 fl oz whipping cream

Salt and pepper

2 tbsps chopped chives

Preparation time: 20 minutes
Cooking time: 25 minutes
Nutritional value:
Analysis per serving, approx:
• 1470kJ/350kcal
• 6g protein
• 17g fat
• 43g carbohydrate

Scrape, wash and dice the carrots. Wash, trim and slice the spring onions. Peel, wash and dice the potatoes. • Melt the margarine in a large saucepan. Add the maple syrup. Toss the sliced onions and diced carrots in this mixture for 5 minutes or until caramelised. Add the potatoes, and top up with the vegetable stock. Cover and simmer for 25 minutes. • Whip the cream until it is stiff. Season the vegetables to taste. Fold in the whipped cream, and sprinkle with the chives. • Potato Croquettes made with cracked wheat (see recipe) make a good accompaniment.

Our Tip: For a low-calorie version, replace the whipped cream with natural thick-set yogurt.

Meatless Vegetable Dishes

Sustaining vegetable meals make a change

Italian-style Pumpkin

Illustrated in background

1 tsp salt
2l/3¹/₂ pints water
1kg/2¹/₄lbs firm pumpkin, peeled
400g/14oz pecorino or feta cheese
200ml/6 fl oz natural thick-set yogurt
4 tbsps chopped chives
4 tbsps wholewheat flour
1 whole egg
1 egg yolk
10 tbsps wholewheat breadcrumbs
6 tbsps olive oil

Cooking time: 50 minutes
Nutritional value:
Analysis per serving, approx:
• 2165kJ/515kcal
• 20g protein
• 36g fat
• 28g carbohydrate

Bring the salted water to the boil. • Cut the peeled pumpkin into even 5mm/¹/₂inch slices and discard the seeds. Blanch the slices in the boiling water, a few at a time, for 5 minutes and drain. • Grate the cheese and mix with the chives and sufficient yogurt for easy spreading. Spread half the pumpkin slices with this mixture and cover with a plain slice to make a 'sandwich'. Coat with flour. Beat the whole egg, egg yolk and 1-2 tbsps yogurt together. Dip the floured pumpkin sandwiches in the egg, then coat with breadcrumbs. Press the crumbs over the surface, and leave to rest for a few minutes. • Heat the oil in a large frying-pan. Fry the pumpkin slices in batches until crisp and golden on both sides. • Keep warm on a preheated dish until all are ready.

Tomato and Leek Scramble

Illustrated in foreground

3 leeks, white parts only
4 beefsteak tomatoes
4 potatoes boiled in their skins (400g/14oz)
1 large onion
3 tbsps sunflower oil
¹/₂ tsp salt
2 eggs
¹/₄ tsp each salt and cayenne pepper
4 tbsps crème fraîche
3 tbsps chopped chives

Preparation time: 20 minutes
Cooking time: 25 minutes
Nutritional value:
Analysis per serving, approx:
• 1405kJ/335kcal
• 14g protein
• 15g fat
• 36g carbohydrate

Thoroughly wash the leeks, dry them and slice them into rings. Skin and peel the tomatoes and slice them crossways into eight wedges, discarding the stalk ends. Peel and slice the potatoes. Peel and chop the onion. • Sauté the chopped onion and leek in the hot oil. Add the potato. Sprinkle with the salt and fry for about 8 minutes, turning occasionally. • Add the tomato, cover, and cook gently for a further 15 minutes. • Beat the eggs, salt, paprika and crème fraîche together, fold into the vegetables and leave in an uncovered pan over a very low heat to set. • Serve from the frying-pan, sprinkled with chives. • Veal cutlets make a good accompaniment.

Our Tip: Use the discarded, dark-green leaves of the leeks - about half the stalk - with carrot, onion, celery and parsnip or turnip to make vegetable stock.

Chinese Leaves, Chinese style

This classic Chinese recipe is surprisingly easy

2 dried Chinese cloud ear mushrooms
1¹/₂kg/3lbs 6oz Chinese leaves
2 green peppers
4 tbsps corn oil
125ml/4 fl oz hot vegetable stock
200g/7oz fresh prawns
1 tbsp cornflour
1 tbsp wine vinegar
2 tbsps soy sauce
Pinch each of salt and sugar

Preparation time: 30 minutes
Cooking time: 25 minutes
Nutritional value:

Analysis per serving, approx:
• 965kJ/230kcal
• 15g protein
• 12g fat
• 15g carbohydrate

Soak the dried mushrooms in hot water for 20 minutes, drain and cut into strips. • Remove green tips of the Chinese leaves and reserve for a salad.

Wash and dry the white stalks and cut into 2cm/³/₄inch slices. Halve the peppers, discard seeds and pith, wash, dry and dice. • Heat half of the oil. Fry the stalks for 5 minutes, add the diced peppers and cook for 3 minutes. Add the vegetable stock, cover, and simmer for about 20 minutes until soft. • Remove the vegetables, reserving the cooking liquid, and keep warm. • Sauté the drained mushrooms and prawns in the remaining oil. Pour the reserved cooking liquid over them, bring to the boil, cover, and cook for 5 minutes over a low heat. • Dissolve the cornflour in the vinegar and soy sauce and use to thicken the sauce. Season to taste with salt and sugar. Add the cooked vegetables and heat through. • Potatoes tossed in parsley or boiled rice make excellent accompaniments.

Chicory with Fish Fillets

An unusual combination

600g/1lb 6oz filleted cod or haddock
1l/1³/₄ pints water
1 tsp salt
1 tbsp lemon juice
¹/₂ bay leaf
2 white peppercorns
800g/1³/₄lbs chicory
2 onions
2 tbsps sunflower oil
125ml/4fl oz single cream
¹/₄ tsp each salt and white pepper
2 tsps mild curry powder
1 tbsp chopped parsley

Preparation time: 15 minutes
Cooking time: 20 minutes
Nutritional value:

Analysis per serving, approx:
• 1345kJ/320kcal
• 32g protein ·
• 17g fat
• 10g carbohydrate

Wash the fish fillets. Bring the water to the boil with the salt, lemon juice, bay leaf and peppercorns. Add the fish, reduce the heat and simmer gently for 8 minutes. • Remove the damaged outer leaves of the chicory and cut a wedge out of the stalk end. Wash, drain and cut into 3cm/1¹/₄ inch strips. Peel and chop the onions. • Remove fish fillets from the stock, and cut into pieces about 4cm/1¹/₂ inches square. Measure out 125ml/4 fl oz of the fish stock. • Heat the oil. Fry the onion until golden. Add the chicory and continue to cook. Pour the measured fish stock over the vegetables and cook, covered, over a low heat for 8 minutes. • Combine the salt, pepper and curry powder with the cream, and mix this with the vegetables. Add the pieces of fish, and reheat the whole dish, but do not let it boil. • Sprinkle with parsley before serving.

Fennel with Ham and Tomato Sauce

A special treat for lovers of Mediterranean cuisine

4 fennel bulbs (about 1kg/2¼lbs)
2 tbsps oil
250ml/8 fl oz chicken stock
125ml/4 fl oz white wine
3 tbsps tomato purée
1 tbsp flour
¼ tsp each dried oregano and dried basil
200g/7oz cooked lean ham
Pinch of white pepper
¼ tsp sugar
2 tbsps freshly grated Parmesan cheese

Preparation time: 10 minutes
Cooking time: 25 minutes
Nutritional value:
Analysis per serving, approx:
- 1510kJ/360kcal
- 18g protein
- 18g fat
- 25g carbohydrate

Remove the outer leaves of the fennel bulbs. Cut off the feathery green leaves, wash, shake dry and chop finely. Cover and set aside. Trim the fennel stalks, and halve the bulbs. • Heat the oil in a heavy casserole dish, and fry the fennel bulbs on both sides until they begin to brown. Heat the chicken stock and pour it and the wine over the fennel. Cover and cook for about 25 minutes. • Lift the tender fennel bulbs out of the stock, and keep them warm. Combine the tomato purée with the flour. Mix this into the braising liquid and boil for 3 minutes, stirring constantly. Crumble the dried herbs and add to the sauce. Finally, add the diced ham and season the sauce to taste with the pepper and sugar. • Pour the sauce over the fennel bulbs, and sprinkle with the Parmesan. • The reserved fennel leaves may be used to flavour boiled rice to accompany this dish.

Fennel with Smoked Pork Loin

A light sauce binds these delicious ingredients

1kg/2¼lbs fennel
1l/1¾ pints slightly salted water
300g/10oz smoked loin of pork
25g/1oz butter
1 tbsp flour
1 tbsp Marsala
4 tbsps single cream
Pinch each of salt and white pepper

Preparation time: 10 minutes
Cooking time: 35 minutes
Nutritional value:
Analysis per serving, approx:
- 1870kJ/445kcal
- 23g protein ·
- 28g fat
- 25g carbohydrate

Discard the outer leaves of the fennel bulbs. Cut off the feathery green leaves, wash, shake dry and chop finely. Cover and set aside. Trim the fennel stalks, quarter the bulbs and cut into strips. Cook fennel in the boiling salted water for about 25 minutes. • Cut the smoked pork into strips of a similar size. Drain the fennel in a colander, reserving 750ml/1¼ pints of the cooking liquid. • Melt the butter in a saucepan and add the flour to make a roux. Gradually add the reserved cooking water, bring to the boil and cook for 5 minutes, stirring vigorously. Add the Marsala and cream, and season to taste with salt and pepper. • Add the fennel and smoked pork to the sauce, and leave for 5 minutes to allow the flavours to combine. • Sprinkle with the fennel green before serving. • Roast potatoes make a good accompaniment.

Baked Salsify

Discover a new delicacy – salsify, the oyster plant

500ml/16 fl oz water
4 tbsps vinegar
2 tbsps flour
1kg/2¼lbs salsify (scorzonera)
1l/1¾ pints water
1 tsp salt • 4 tbsps lemon juice
1 onion
200g/7oz cooked lean ham
5 tomatoes
15g/½oz butter
1 tsp anchovy paste or 1 mashed anchovy fillet
Pinch each of white pepper and grated nutmeg
Dash of Worcestershire sauce
½ tsp dried basil
100g/4oz grated Cheddar cheese

Preparation time: 10 minutes
Cooking time: 45-50 minutes
Nutritional value:
Analysis per serving, approx:
- 2165kJ/515kcal
- 22g protein
- 22g fat
- 57g carbohydrate

Stir the vinegar and flour into the water. • Scrub the salsify under running water. Peel it, trim the ends and any dark patches, rinse again and immediately drop into the flour-and-water mixture to prevent discolouration. • Bring the extra 1l/1½ pints water to the boil with the salt and lemon juice. Add the salsify and simmer for 35-40 minutes. • Peel and chop the onion, and dice the ham. Skin and chop the tomatoes. • Preheat the oven to 220°C/430°F/Gas Mark 7. • Fry the diced onion and ham in the melted butter. Add the chopped tomatoes, anchovy paste, seasonings and dried basil. • Drain the salsify, reserving the cooking liquid, and arrange in an ovenproof dish. Measure out 125ml/4 fl oz of the reserved liquid and stir it into the tomato sauce; pour this over the salsify and sprinkle with the cheese. • Bake on the middle shelf of the oven for 10 minutes.

Delicious Stuffed Cabbage

Minced lamb or poultry make tempting stuffings

White Cabbage with Lamb
Illustrated on the left

1 white cabbage (800g/1³/₄lbs)
1 tsp salt
2 onions • 1 clove garlic
500g/1lb 2oz minced leg of lamb
100g/4oz cooked brown rice
1 egg • 1 tsp lemon juice
¹/₂ tsp dried thyme
Pinch of salt and white pepper
1 bunch parsley • 1 bay leaf
2 tbsps sunflower oil
250ml/8 fl oz hot vegetable stock
Sprig of fresh rosemary
1 tbsp wholewheat flour
100ml/3 fl oz crème fraîche

Preparation time: 20 minutes
Cooking time: 1 hour
Nutritional value:
Analysis per serving, approx:
• 2375 kJ/565 kcal • 30g protein
• 39g fat • 23g carbohydrate

Remove a wedge from the stalk end of the cabbage. Blanch the cabbage for 10 minutes in boiling salted water. • Peel the onions and garlic, chop them finely and combine with the meat, rice, egg and seasonings. • Flatten 16 large cabbage leaves, slitting the stalk if necessary. Arrange the cabbage leaves in pairs, one on top of another, and divide the stuffing between the 8 double leaves. Fold the leaves over the stuffing to make neat parcels and tie with kitchen thread. • Shred the remaining cabbage leaves. Coarsely chop the bunch of parsley, but reserve 2 tablespoons of finely-chopped parsley for the garnish. • Fry the cabbage rolls in the heated oil. Add the parsley, the shredded cabbage, the bay leaf, the vegetable stock and the rosemary. Gently braise over a low heat, covered, for 50 minutes. Remove the cabbage parcels to a heated dish and keep warm.Combine the crème fraîche with the flour and use the mixture to thicken the sauce • Pour the sauce over the stuffed cabbage leaves and garnish with parsley.

Red Cabbage with Chicken
Illustrated on the right

1 red cabbage (800g/1³/₄lbs)
1 tsp salt • 1 tbsp vinegar
500g/1lb 2oz chicken breast
1 day-old bread roll
50g/2oz streaky bacon
1 onion • 1 carrot
15g/¹/₂oz butter
Pinch of ground cloves
3 tbsps oil
125ml/4fl oz dry red wine
125ml/4fl oz hot vegetable stock
Salt and pepper
1-2 tsps redcurrant jelly

Preparation time: 30 minutes
Cooking time: 55 minutes
Nutritional value:
Analysis per serving, approx:
• 1765kJ/420kcal • 35g protein
• 19g fat
• 20g carbohydrate

Prepare cabbage following the instructions in the previous recipe. Add the vinegar to the salted water, bring to the boil and blanch the cabbage for 15 minutes. Select and prepare 16 large leaves. • Preheat the oven to 200°C/400°F/Gas Mark 6. • Chop or mince the chicken finely. Soak the bread roll in cold water and squeeze out the excess moisture. Chop the bacon, onion and carrot, and sauté in the butter. Add the seasoning, the bread and the chicken. Make 'parcels' following the instructions in the previous recipe. Fry in the oil. • Pour the red wine over the stuffed cabbage leaves, and bake for 40 minutes. • Pour the vegetable stock into the cooking dish. Season with the salt and pepper and flavour with redcurrant jelly.

Interesting Winter Vegetables

Kale and swede need the right accompaniments

Kale, French Style
Illustrated in background

1kg/2¼lbs kale
2l/3½ pints water
1 tsp salt
2 onions
50g/2oz butter
500ml/16 fl oz hot strong beef stock
½ tsp salt
Pinch each of black pepper and chilli powder
1l/1¾ pints water
400g/14oz chestnuts
1 tbsp sugar
125ml/4 fl oz single cream

Preparation time: 15 minutes
Cooking time: 1½ hours
Nutritional value:
Analysis per serving, approx:
- 2350kJ/560kcal
- 20g protein
- 23g fat
- 68g carbohydrate

Discard the tough kale stems and blanch the leaves in boiling salted water for 5 minutes. Then drain, cool, and chop coarsely. • Peel and chop the onions and sauté in half the butter. Add the kale, beef stock and seasoning. Simmer, covered, for 1½ hours. • Meanwhile, make a deep crosswise incision at the pointed end of each chestnut and boil briskly for 20-25 minutes in 1l/1¾ pints water. • Peel the chestnuts while still hot. • Melt the rest of the butter, sprinkle in sugar and allow to caramelise, stirring frequently. Toss the chestnuts in this mixture, and keep hot in a covered pan over a very low heat. • Mix the cooked, drained kale with the cream, check the seasoning, and combine with the chestnuts. • Boiled potatoes go well with this.

Swede with Lamb Chops
Illustrated in foreground

1½kg/3lbs 6oz swede
3 onions
2 tbsps lard
1 tbsp sugar
500ml/16 fl oz hot beef stock
½ tsp salt
¼ tsp white pepper
1 tsp dried marjoram
1 tbsp chopped parsley
4 lamb chops, each weighing 100g/4oz
2 tbsps oil
Salt and pepper

Preparation time: 15 minutes
Cooking time: 45 minutes
Nutritional value:
Analysis per serving, approx:
- 2835kJ/675kcal·
- 20g protein
- 44g fat
- 49g carbohydrate

Scrub the swede under cold running water. Peel it, removing any woody parts. Dry it and dice it. Peel and chop the onions. • Heat the lard. Fry the onion until transparent. Add the swede, and sprinkle with sugar; stir continuously until the sugar caramelises. Pour the beef stock over the vegetables. Mix in the salt, pepper and marjoram, cover and braise for 45 minutes. • Sprinkle the vegetables with parsley before serving. • Wash and dry the lamb chops, and make several incisions round the edges to prevent them from curling up during cooking. Fry in hot oil for 4 minutes on each side, then season. • Mashed potatoes make a good accompaniment.

Bean and Beef Casserole

Tastes best with young beans

Cucumber Casserole with Chicken Dumplings

A delicious combination

Bean and Beef Casserole
500g/1lb 2oz green beans
500g/1lb 2oz potatoes
2 onions
600g/1lb 6oz brisket of beef
2 tbsps oil
250ml/8 fl oz hot beef stock
$\frac{1}{2}$ tsp salt
$\frac{1}{4}$ tsp white pepper
3 tbsps tomato purée
2 sprigs savory
500g/1lb 2oz tomatoes
$\frac{1}{2}$ tsp dried rosemary
2 tbsps chopped parsley

Preparation time: 30 minutes
Cooking time: 45 minutes
Nutritional value:
Analysis per serving, approx:
- 1930kJ/460kcal
- 39g protein
- 17g fat
- 38g carbohydrate

String the beans if necessary. Rinse in cold water and cut into 4cm/1½-inch pieces. Peel, wash and dice the potatoes. Peel and chop the onions. Wash and dry the meat and cut it into even-sized cubes. • Heat the oil in a large saucepan. Fry the onion until transparent. Add the meat and brown on all sides, turning from time to time, for 7-8 minutes. Pour the beef stock over the meat. Stir in the salt, pepper and tomato purée. Add the savory and cook, covered, for 15 minutes. • Add the beans and potato to the meat and continue cooking for another 20 minutes. • Meanwhile, skin and quarter the tomatoes, removing the hard stalk ends, and cut the quarters in half again. Add the tomatoes and rosemary to the vegetables and continue cooking for 10 minutes more. • Remove the savory, and serve sprinkled with the parsley

Cucumber Casserole with Chicken Dumplings
1kg/2¼lbs cucumbers, ridge if available
500g/1lb 2oz potatoes
2 onions
2 cloves garlic
600g/1lb 6oz chicken breasts, skinned and boned
Pinch cayenne pepper
1 egg
5 tbsps wholewheat breadcrumbs
2 tbsps sunflower oil
500ml/16fl oz hot vegetable stock
Salt and black pepper
2 tbsps tomato ketchup
4 tbsps crème fraîche
2 tbsps chopped parsley

Preparation time: 20 minutes
Cooking time: 30 minutes
Nutritional value:
Analysis per serving, approx:
- 1955kJ/465kcal
- 45g protein
- 13g fat
- 42g carbohydrate

Peel the cucumbers, halve them lengthways, scrape out the seeds, and slice them. Peel, wash and dice the potatoes. Peel the onions and garlic and chop finely. • Mince the chicken, season with salt and cayenne pepper, and combine with the egg and breadcrumbs to make a dough. Cover the dough with a damp cloth and leave to rest. • Heat the oil. Fry the onion and garlic until transparent. Add the cucumber, and sauté, stirring occasionally. Then mix in the potato and add the vegetable stock. Cover the pan and cook for 30 minutes. • Shape the minced chicken mixture into walnut-sized balls and poach in simmering, salted water for 10 minutes. • Season the vegetables to taste with salt and pepper, and add the ketchup and crème fraîche. Remove the dumplings with a slotted spoon and arrange on top of the vegetables. Sprinkle with the parsley.

Delicious Ways of Serving Root Vegetables

Fresh herbs enhance the flavour of this highly nutritious dish

Young Turnip and Chicken Casserole
Illustrated on the right

| 1kg/2¼lbs young turnips |
| 1 packet mixed potherbs (celery, leek, carrot, parsley) |
| 750ml/1¼ pints vegetable stock |
| 4 chicken legs each weighing 180g/6oz |
| 600g/1lb 6oz floury potatoes |
| ½ tsp salt |
| ¼ tsp each white pepper and cayenne |
| 4 shallots |
| 2 tbsps corn oil |
| 2 tbsps chopped sage or parsley |

Preparation time: 10 minutes
Cooking time: 40 minutes
Nutritional value:
Analysis per serving, approx:
- 1805kJ/430kcal
- 44g protein
- 12g fat
- 36g carbohydrate

Peel, wash and dry the turnips, and cut into 2.5cm/1in cubes. Trim and wash the potherbs and chop them coarsely . Put the turnips and other vegetables in a saucepan with the vegetable stock, bring to the boil, cover and cook for 20 minutes. • Wash and dry the chicken legs. Peel, wash and dice the potatoes. Add the chicken legs, diced potato, salt, pepper and cayenne to the turnips, mixing well. Cover and cook for a further 20 minutes. • Peel the shallots and cut into thin rings. Heat the oil. Fry the shallots until golden, and garnish the casserole with these and the herbs before serving.

Kohlrabi Stew with Cheese
Illustrated on the left

| 4 kohlrabi (800g/1¾lbs) |
| 2 onions |
| 500g/1lb 2oz new potatoes |
| 2 tbsps oil |
| 250ml/8 fl oz vegetable stock |
| 1 tbsp flour |
| ½ tsp salt |
| Pinch each of white pepper and sugar |
| 2 egg yolks |
| 125ml/4 fl oz single cream |
| 100g/4oz Gouda cheese, freshly grated |
| 4 tbsps chopped fresh lovage or marjoram |

Preparation time: 20 minutes
Cooking time: 30 minutes
Nutritional value:
Analysis per serving, approx:
- 1890kJ/450kcal
- 16g protein
- 26g fat
- 38g carbohydrate

Peel and wash the kohlrabi and cut it into fingers. Wash, dry and chop the tender green leaves; cover and set aside. Peel and chop the onions. Scrub the potatoes but do not peel them. Boil for 30 minutes. • Heat the oil. Sauté the onion until transparent. Add the kohlrabi, sauté briefly, and pour 125ml/4fl oz vegetable stock over the vegetables. Braise over a low heat for 15 minutes in a covered saucepan. • Mix the flour with the rest of the cold vegetable stock, making sure there are no lumps, and use this to thicken the sauce. Continue cooking the vegetables in the sauce for a few more minutes, stirring occasionally. • Drain the potatoes, skin and slice, then mix them with the sauce. Season to taste with the salt, pepper and sugar. • Combine the egg yolks, cream and cheese, and stir this mixture into the vegetables. Sprinkle with the lovage and chopped kohlrabi greens before serving. • Croquettes make a good accompaniment.

Stuffed Spinach Rolls

A meatless spinach delicacy

400g/14oz button mushrooms
30g/1oz butter
1/4 tsp salt
Dash of Tabasco sauce
125ml/4 fl oz vegetable stock
50g/2oz crustless white bread
1 egg
600g/1lb 6oz large spinach leaves, or Swiss chard
1 onion
1/4 tsp salt
Pinch of grated nutmeg
100g/4oz crème fraîche
2 tbsps freshly grated Parmesan cheese

Preparation time: 45 minutes
Cooking time: 15 minutes
Nutritional value:
Analysis per serving, approx:
- 1175kJ/280kcal
- 13g protein
- 17g fat
- 19g carbohydrate

Trim, wash and chop the mushrooms, and sauté in half the butter; season with salt and Tabasco sauce. Add 6 tbsps vegetable stock and cook gently, uncovered, for 5 minutes. • Crumble the white bread, and moisten with the rest of the vegetable stock. Add the breadcrumb mixture to the mushrooms. Mix in the egg, and set the stuffing on one side. • Trim the thick stalks from the spinach leaves, wash and blanch for 5 minutes in boiling salted water. Drain and pat the leaves dry, and make eight 10 x 15-cm/4 x 6-inch rectangles, using several leaves for each. Coarsely chop the remaining spinach. • Peel and finely chop the onions and sauté in the rest of the butter until transparent. Add the chopped spinach, season with salt and nutmeg, cook briefly, then use to line the bottom of an ovenproof dish. • Preheat the oven to 200°C/400°F/Gas Mark 6. • Divide the filling among the spinach rectangles, roll them up, turning the ends under. Lay them on the bed of spinach in the dish. Spread over the crème fraîche and then the cheese. • Bake for 15 minutes. • Serve with potato pancakes.

Asparagus Bake

It is impossible to have asparagus too often!

1kg/2¼lbs asparagus
1 tsp salt
1 sugar lump
200g/7oz lean cooked ham
15g/½oz butter
1 tbsp flour
125ml/4fl oz milk
½ tsp salt
¼ tsp each white pepper and hot paprika
100g/4oz hard yellow cheese, freshly grated
2 egg yolks
Butter to grease the dish

Preparation time: 30 minutes
Cooking time: 30 minutes
Nutritional value:
Analysis per serving, approx:
• 1555kJ/370kcal
• 25g protein
• 24g fat
• 13g carbohydrate

Peel the asparagus cut off the woody ends. Tie in four bundles. Bring the water to the boil with the salt and sugar. Add asparagus, cover and simmer for 10 minutes. • Cut the ham into julienne strips. • Butter a shallow ovenproof dish. Preheat the oven to 200°C/400°F/Gas Mark 6. • Drain the asparagus, reserving 125ml/4 fl oz of the cooking liquid, and remove string. Arrange in the ovenproof dish, topped with the strips of ham. • Melt the butter in a saucepan, add the flour, and cook until golden, stirring continuously. Stir in the reserved cooking water and the milk. Mix in the salt, pepper and paprika, and simmer for 5 minutes, stirring constantly. Stir in the grated cheese. Remove the sauce from the heat and allow it to cool slightly, then mix in the egg yolks, and pour the sauce over the asparagus. Bake for 20 minutes. • A tomato salad with onions and chives makes a good accompaniment.

Courgette Bake with a Grain Topping

The subtle flavour of this dish depends on the herbs

1 onion
2 cloves garlic
600g/1lb 6oz beef tomatoes
50g/2oz young dandelion leaves
3 tbsps sunflower oil
1 tsp salt
1 tsp chopped rosemary
1 tsp honey
Pinch of cayenne
1kg/2¼lbs courgettes
100g/4oz crème fraîche
200g/7oz rye flakes

Preparation time: 30 minutes
Cooking time: 20 minutes
Nutritional value:
Analysis per serving, approx:
• 1575kJ/375kcal
• 13g protein
• 11g fat
• 55g carbohydrate

Peel and finely chop the onion and garlic. Skin and chop the tomatoes finely, discarding the hard stalk ends. Wash the dandelion leaves, shake them dry and shred them. • Heat 1 tbsp oil. Sauté the onion and garlic until transparent. Add the chopped tomatoes. Season with the salt, rosemary, honey and cayenne, and cook uncovered over a low heat for 10 minutes, stirring frequently. Then mix in the dandelion leaves. • Wash and dry the courgettes, cut off the stalk ends, and cut into 2cm/¾-inch dice. Fry the courgettes in the remaining oil until golden on all sides. • Preheat the oven to 200°C/400°F/Gas Mark 6. • Mix the rye flakes into the crème fraîche. Arrange the courgettes and the tomato sauce in alternate layers in an ovenproof dish, then spread the grain topping over the vegetables. • Bake on the middle shelf of the oven for 20 minutes.

Tomato and Egg Bake

Also makes a light, attractive entrée

Potato and Ham Bake

A meal in itself - serve with a mixed salad

Tomato and Egg Bake

2 slices of wholemeal bread
25g/1oz butter
500g/1lb 2oz button mushrooms
2 onions
1 large clove garlic
1 tsp salt
1/4 tsp black pepper
2 tbsps parsley, chopped
4 eggs, hard-boiled
4 large tomatoes
125ml/4fl oz natural thick-set yogurt
3 tbsps hard yellow cheese, freshly grated

Preparation time: 15 minutes
Cooking time: 30 minutes
Nutritional value:
Analysis per serving, approx:
- 1240kJ/495kcal
- 16g fat
- 20g carbohydrate

Cut the bread into small even squares, fry until crisp in 1 tbsp butter and place in an ovenproof dish. Trim, wash and finely slice the mushrooms. Peel and chop the onions and garlic and sauté in the remaining butter until transparent. Add the mushrooms, salt and pepper, and for 8 minutes. • Add half the parsley to the mushrooms, and arrange on top of of fried bread squares. • Preheat the oven to 200°C/400°F/Gas Mark 6. • Shell and slice the eggs, and arrange on top of the mushrooms. Skin and slice the tomatoes, and arrange in a ring round the edge of the dish. Stir the grated cheese into the natural yogurt and pour over the sliced egg. Cook on the middle shelf of the oven for 20 minutes. • Shortly before serving sprinkle with the rest of the chopped parsley. • A crisp green salad and French bread go well with this.

Potato and Ham Bake

800g/1³/₄lbs floury potatoes
300g/10oz lean cooked ham
25g/1oz butter • 1 tbsp flour
500ml/16 fl oz warm milk
1/2 tsp salt
1/4 tsp white pepper
Pinch of grated nutmeg
2 egg yolks
3 tbsps freshly crushed cracked wheat
50g/2oz Emmental cheese, grated
1 large onion
4 tbsps chopped parsley
l tomato

Preparation time: 10 minutes
Cooking time: 55 minutes
Nutritional value:
Analysis per serving, approx:
- 2435kJ/580kcal
- 29g protein
- 31g fat
- 46g carbohydrate

Scrub the potatoes under cold running water. Boil for 30 minutes, allow to cool, peel, and dice. • Preheat the oven to 220°C/430°F/Gas Mark 7. • Dice the ham and mix with the potatoes. • Melt half the butter in a saucepan. Sprinkle with the flour and cook until golden, stirring constantly. Add the milk gradually, stirring briskly, and allow the sauce to boil for a few minutes. • Season the sauce with salt, pepper and nutmeg, remove from the heat and allow to cool slightly before mixing in the egg yolks. • Combine the potato and ham with the sauce and pour into an ovenproof dish. Mix the cracked wheat with the grated cheese and sprinkle over the potato mixture. • Bake on the lowest shelf of the oven for 25 minutes. • Meanwhile, peel the onions and slice them into rings. Heat the remaining butter, and fry the onion gently until golden. • Garnish the dish with the fried onion rings, chopped parsley and a tomato cut into wedges.

Cauliflower à la Belle Melusine

Cauliflower cooked in a clay brick, an unglazed earthenware pot

1 cauliflower (about 1kg/2¼lbs)
500g/1lb 2oz tomatoes
½ bread roll
250g/9oz each minced beef and pork
2 small onions
2 eggs
½ tsp pepper
1 tsp salt
100g/4oz Parmesan cheese, freshly grated
4 tbsps butter
2 tbsps chopped parsley

Preparation time: 20 minutes
Cooking time: 1 hour
Nutritional value:
Analysis per serving, approx:
• 2630kj/625kcal
• 39g protein
• 35g fat
• 19g carbohydrate

Soak a clay brick in cold water for 20 minutes. • Trim the cauliflower and cut it into florets. Wash the florets. Skin and quarter the tomatoes, discarding the hard stalk ends. Soak the bread in cold water. Peel and chop the onions, and combine them with the eggs, pepper, ½ tsp salt and the mince in a bowl. Squeeze any excess moisture out of the roll, and add to other ingredients. Mix well. • Arrange the cauliflower florets and the mince in alternating layers in the soaked clay pot, finishing with a layer of mince. Arrange the tomato sections on top and season with salt. Sprinkle with the grated Parmesan and dot with butter. • Cover the pot, and place on the bottom shelf of a cold oven. Set the oven at 220°C/430°F/Gas Mark 7. Cook for 1 hour. • Before serving, sprinkle with parsley. • Freshly-baked French bread or mashed potato make equally good accompaniments for this.

Crusty Toppings Straight from the Oven

Exotic recipes but with familiar flavours

Sweetcorn Bake from Chile
Illustrated in background

75g/3oz sultanas
3 large onions
2 tbsps sunflower oil
400g/1 lb each minced beef and pork
125-250ml/4-8oz beef stock
1 tsp salt
Few dashes Tabasco sauce
1kg/2¼lbs canned sweetcorn
¼ tsp each salt and sugar
50g/2oz butter
1 tbsp chopped parsley

Preparation time: 30 minutes
Cooking time: 40 minutes
Nutritional value:
Analysis per serving, approx:
• 2960kJ/705kcal
• 34g protein
• 40g fat
• 52g carbohydrate

Wash the sultanas in hot water, and soak them in lukewarm water for 20 minutes. Peel the onions and chop them finely . • Heat the oil. Sauté the onion until golden. Add the mince and brown, stirring constantly, then mix in some beef stock, and season well with salt and Tabasco. Drain the sultanas and add to the mince. • Turn into an ovenproof dish. Preheat the oven to 200°C/400°F/Gas Mark 6. • Purée the sweetcorn, and drain in a fine sieve. Season to taste with salt and sugar. Top the mince with the puréed sweetcorn and finally dabs of butter. • Cook in the oven for about 40 minutes. • Before serving, sprinkle with the chopped parsley.

Our Tip: Fresh cranberries or pomegranate seeds may be substituted for the sultanas.

Leeks au Gratin
Front illustration

400g/14oz boiled brisket or silverside of beef
1kg/2¼lbs leeks
1 tsp salt
500g/1lb 2oz potatoes
6 tbsps butter
2 egg yolks
Salt and white pepper
Pinch of grated nutmeg
125ml/4fl oz boiling hot milk
2 tbsps chopped parsley
5 tbsps natural thick-set yogurt
5 tbsps breadcrumbs
Butter to grease the dish

Preparation time: 20 minutes
Cooking time: 1 hour
Nutritional value:
Analysis per serving, approx:
• 2120kJ/505kcal
• 32g protein
• 24g fat
• 40g carbohydrate

Cut the meat into small cubes. Trim the roots and dark green leaves from the leeks. Cut them in half lengthways, wash them and cut into 3cm/1¼-inch lengths. Blanch the leeks in salted water for 10 minutes, then drain. • Peel, wash and dice the potatoes and boil, covered, for 25-30 minutes or until soft. • Drain the potatoes, allowing the steam to evaporate, mash, and incorporate 2 tbsps butter, the egg yolks, salt, pepper, nutmeg and milk, beating hard with an egg whisk. • Preheat the oven to 200°C/400°F/Gas Mark 6. • Butter an ovenproof dish. Put the potato purée into the dish, and top with 2 tbsps butter. Bake in the oven for 15 minutes. • Arrange the meat, leeks and parsley on top of the mashed potato, and pour over the yogurt over the dish. Return to oven for another 5 minutes. • Fry the breadcrumbs in the remaining butter until golden, and sprinkle over the gratin topping.

Leek Risotto

This dish can be adapted for many other types of vegetables

1kg/2¼lbs leeks
400g/14oz tomatoes
1 large onion
50g/2oz streaky bacon
2 tbsps butter
200g/7oz rice
500ml/16 fl oz beef stock
½ tsp salt
¼ tsp black pepper
A pinch of dried thyme
2 tbsps chopped parsley
Grated Parmesan (optional)

Preparation time: 30 minutes
Cooking time: 20-25 minutes
Nutritional value:
Analysis per serving, approx:
• 1765kJ/420kcal
• 11g protein
• 15g fat
• 60g carbohydrate

Trim the dark green leaves and roots from the leeks. Halve the stems lengthways, wash thoroughly and cut into thin slices.

Skin and quarter the tomatoes, removing the hard stalk ends, and cut into large cubes. Peel and finely chop the onion. Dice the bacon. • Melt the butter in a large saucepan. Sauté the chopped onion until transparent, add the rice, and cook gently until translucent. Heat the beef stock. Add the sliced leek to the rice, sauté briefly, then add the beef stock. Cook over a gentle heat for 20-25 minutes, adding more water if necessary. • 15 minutes into the cooking time, mix in the tomato and season to taste with the salt, pepper and thyme. Continue cooking until rice is soft. Fry the diced bacon in a small, dry frying-pan until crisp, and mix into the risotto. Just before serving sprinkle with the parsley. • Grated Parmesan may also be served with this, if desired.

Aubergine and Rice Bake

The minced meat can be replaced by feta cheese

200g/7oz long-grain rice
2 l/3½ pints water
1 tsp salt
500g/1lb 2oz aubergines
1 tsp salt
2 onions
1 clove garlic
3 tbsps sunflower oil
200g/7oz each minced beef and pork
¼ tsp each salt, black pepper and sweet paprika
½ tsp dried basil
4 tomatoes
125ml/4 fl oz vegetable stock
2 tbsps chopped parsley

Preparation time: 30 minutes
Cooking time: 30 minutes
Nutritional value:
Analysis per serving, approx:
• 2540kJ/605kcal
• 29g protein
• 28g fat
• 60g carbohydrate

Boil the rice in the salted water for 15 minutes. • Wash and dry the aubergines, removing the stems. Cut into round slices, sprinkle with salt and leave to stand for 15 minutes. • Peel and finely chop the onions and garlic. • Sauté the chopped onion and garlic in 1 tbsp heated oil until transparent. Add the mince and fry, stirring constantly, until well browned. Season with the salt, pepper, paprika and basil. • Pat the slices of aubergine dry, and fry on both sides in plenty of oil. • Preheat the oven to 200°C/400°F/Gas Mark 6. • Drain the rice. Put half the rice in an ovenproof dish. Follow with half the aubergines, then all the mince, followed by the remaining aubergines, and lastly the rest of the rice. Wash, dry and slice the tomatoes and arrange them over the rice. Pour the vegetable stock over the entire dish. • Cook in the oven for 30 minutes. • Serve sprinkled with parsley.

Brussels Sprout Bake

A delicious vegetable dish

800g/1³/₄lbs Brussels sprouts

2l/3¹/₂ pints water

1 tsp salt

350g/11oz lean cooked ham

125ml/4 fl oz hot beef stock

3 eggs

125ml/4 fl oz milk

1 tsp salt

¹/₄ tsp white pepper

Pinch of grated nutmeg

100g/4oz Gouda cheese, freshly grated

Preparation time: 10 minutes
Cooking time: 35 minutes
Nutritional value:
Analysis per serving, approx:
• 2185kJ/520kcal
• 39g protein
• 33g fat
• 16g carbohydrate

Trim and wash the Brussels sprouts. Bring the salted water to the boil, add the Brussels sprouts, cover and cook on low heat for 10 minutes. Drain and rinse under a cold tap. • Slice the ham into strips. • Put the Brussels sprouts and half of the ham in an ovenproof dish and pour the hot beef stock over them. • Preheat the oven to 220°C/430°F/Gas Mark 7. • Beat the eggs with the milk, salt, pepper and nutmeg, and pour this mixture over the Brussels sprouts. Arrange the remaining strips of a ham in the centre of the dish, and sprinkle with the cheese. • Cover with aluminium foil and bake for 15 minutes on the middle shelf of the oven.• Then remove the foil, and cook, uncovered, for a further 10 minutes. • Fresh crusty bread or roast potatoes make good accompaniments.

Pepper Bake

Tasty and filling with either red or green peppers

800g/1³/₄lbs floury potatoes

150g mortadella sausage

2 cloves garlic

1 tbsp sunflower oil

2 tbsps chopped parsley

4 green peppers (800g/1³/₄lbs)

2 eggs

125ml/4 fl oz milk

¹/₂ tsp salt

¹/₄ tsp white pepper

Bunch of mixed herbs, e.g. oregano, sage, thyme

50g/2oz Parmesan cheese,freshly grated

1 tbsp sunflower oil

Preparation time: 20 minutes
Cooking time: 1 hour 10 minutes
Nutritional value:
Analysis per serving, approx:
• 2035kJ/485kcal
• 21g protein
• 25g fat
• 43g carbohydrate

Boil the potatoes, unpeeled, until cooked; drain and cool. • Dice the sausage. Peel and finely chop the garlic. • Heat the oil. Sauté the mortadella and chopped garlic until crisp and brown. Mix in the parsley, and set aside. • Quarter the peppers, remove the pith and seeds, wash, dry and cut into strips. Peel and slice the potatoes. • Preheat the oven to 220°C/430°F/Gas Mark 7. • Beat the eggs with the milk, salt and pepper. • Alternate layers of sliced potato, strips of pepper and sausage mixture in an ovenproof dish. Pour the egg and milk mixture over them. • Cover the dish with aluminium foil and bake on the middle shelf of the oven for 30 minutes. • Meanwhile, wash the herbs, shake them dry, and chop finely. • After 30 minutes scatter with the chopped herbs and Parmesan, and sprinkle with the oil. • Remove the foil and return to the oven for another 5 minutes.

Tasty Winter Hotpots

Something warming for a cold winter day

Salsify and Chicken Hotpot

Illustrated on the left

| 1 chicken weighing about 1kg/2¼lbs, with giblets |
| 1 packet potherbs (celery, leek, carrot, parsley) |
| 2l/3½pints water |
| 1 onion • 1 bay leaf |
| 2 cloves |
| 800g/1¾lbs salsify |
| 6 tbsps vinegar |
| 4 potatoes (400g/14oz) |
| 2 tbsps flour • 4 tbsps milk |
| 2 tbsps capers, drained and rinsed |
| 125ml/4 fl oz plain thick yogurt |
| Salt and white pepper |
| Dash of Worcestershire sauce |
| 4 tbsps chopped chives |

Preparation time: 30 minutes
Cooking time: 1½ hours
Nutritional value:
Analysis per serving, approx:
• 2710kJ/645kcal • 59g protein
• 19g fat • 59g carbohydrate

Wash the chicken in cold water. Wash, trim and coarsely chop the potherbs. • Bring the salted water to the boil and add the chicken, with the heart and liver, and the potherbs. During the first 15 minutes skim off any scum that forms. • Peel the onion, and stick the bay leaf and cloves into it. Add the onion to the chicken, and simmer gently for another 30 minutes. • Scrub the salsify, peel and rinse again. Add a few drops of vinegar to a bowl of cold water and drop the peeled salsify into it as it is peeled, to prevent discolouration. Drain the salsify and cut it into 5cm/2-inch lengths, and cook with the chicken for 30 minutes or until tender. • Peel, wash and dice the potatoes, and cook with the chicken for 20 minutes. • Lift the chicken out of the pot, skin, and bone it and cut into pieces. • Strain off 250ml/8 fl oz of the cooking stock. (Keep the rest to use for soup.) • Mix the flour with the milk, stirring until smooth. Add the measured stock and cook for 10 minutes, stirring constantly. • Reheat the chicken pieces, potatoes, salsify and capers in the sauce. Stir in the yogurt and seasoning. • Sprinkle with chives before serving.

Sweet-and-sour Lentil Hotpot

Illustrated on the right

| 350g/11oz lentils |
| 1½ l/2½ pints water |
| 4 shallots |
| 1 large carrot |
| 400g/14oz floury potatoes |
| 2 tbsps each butter and caster sugar |
| 3 smoked sausages (300g/9oz) |
| ½ tsp salt |
| 2 tbsps vinegar |

Preparation time: 10 minutes
Cooking time: 1 hour

Nutritional value:
Analysis per serving, approx:
• 2940kJ/700kcal
• 33g protein
• 30g fat
• 74g carbohydrate

Wash the lentils in a bowl of cold water, pick them over and remove any that float to the top. Drain in a colander, and boil, uncovered, in the water over a low heat for 30 minutes. • Peel and chop the shallots, carrot and potatoes. • Cook the butter and sugar until caramelised, stirring constantly. Toss the shallots and carrot in this mixture. Add the lentils and their cooking water to the vegetables. Then add the potatoes and the sausage slices. Simmer for 30 minutes. • Flavour with the salt, vinegar and a pinch of caster sugar to produce a potent sweet-and-sour effect.

Dried Peas and Beans: Traditional Cold Weather Food

Dried peas and beans are especially good with herbs and fresh vegetables

Casserole of Peas with Bacon
Illustrated in background

400g/14oz dried green peas
2l/3½ pints water
500g/1lb 2oz floury potatoes
2 leeks
200g/7oz celery
½ tsp each dried savory and thyme
¼ tsp white pepper
½-1 tsp salt
2 onions
100g/4oz streaky bacon

Soaking time: 12 hours
Preparation time: 15 minutes
Cooking time: 2 hours
Nutritional value:
Analysis per serving, approx:
• 2690kJ/640kcal
• 30g protein
• 18g fat
• 89g carbohydrate

Wash and pick over the dried peas, and soak for 12 hours in water to cover. • Then bring the peas to the boil in the water and boil gently for 1½ hours. • Peel, wash and dice the potatoes. Halve the leeks lengthways and wash them, discarding the dark green parts and slicing the white part thinly. Remove and reserve the celery leaves and set aside. Wash and finely dice the celery. After the dried peas have been cooking for 1½ hours, add all the remaining ingredients except the onion and bacon and continue cooking for another 30 minutes. • Meanwhile, peel the onions and slice them into rings. • Fry the bacon rashers in a dry frying-pan until crisp. Sauté the onion rings in the bacon fat until golden. Serve the beans garnished with the onion rings, the bacon and chopped celery leaves.

Beans with Garlic Croutons
Illustrated in foreground

350 white haricot beans
1½ l/2 ½ pints water
2 large onions (about 400g/14oz)
3 cloves garlic
2 heads celery
2 large carrots
2 tbsps olive oil
Salt and white pepper
Pinch of dried marjoram
2 slices wholemeal bread
2 tbsps vegetable margarine
1 tbsp each chopped thyme and chopped parsley

Soaking time: 12 hours
Preparation time: 10 minutes
Cooking time: 2 hours
Nutritional value:
Analysis per serving, approx:
• 2015kJ/480kcal
• 23g protein
• 11g fat
• 72g carbohydrate

Wash the beans, pick them over and soak for 12 hours in the water. • Bring to the boil in fresh water and cook for 1½ hours over a low heat until tender. • Peel and chop the onions and 2 cloves of garlic. Cut the celery into thin slices. Scrape, wash and dice the carrots. • Sauté the vegetables in the oil for 5 minutes, then add to the beans. • Season the beans with the salt, pepper and marjoram and cook, covered, for another 30 minutes. • Peel the remaining clove of garlic, and crush in a garlic press. Cut each slice of bread into 12 squares. • Combine the margarine with the crushed garlic, thyme and parsley. Spread the bread squares with this mixture. • Preheat the oven to 220°C/430°F/Gas Mark 7 • Bake the bread squares until crisp, and arrange over the beans before serving.

Salads and Attractive Accompaniments

The selection covers every season, including vegetables from exotic climes now available in our shops throughout the year

Mixed Salad Platter

A refreshing side-dish or a light supper

1 celeriac
250g/8oz cauliflower
4 small tomatoes
300g/10oz cucumber
4 small carrots
1 red pepper
1 onion
100g/4oz lamb's lettuce
100g/4oz radicchio
12 stuffed olives
¹/₂ tsp coarsely ground black pepper
4 tbsps olive oil
3 tbsps wine vinegar
¹/₂ tsp salt
1 tbsp freshly chopped mixed herbs
1 pot natural yogurt (150g/5¹/₂oz)
1 hard-boiled egg

Preparation time: 20 minutes
Cooking time: 20 minutes
Nutritional value:
Analysis per serving, approx:
- 1115kJ/265kcal
- 9g protein
- 15g fat
- 24g carbohydrate

Wash the celeriac and cook for 20 minutes in water to cover in a saucepan with the lid on. Drain. • Break the cauliflower into florets and boil in salted water for 10 minutes. • Wash, dry and quarter the tomatoes. Wash and slice the cucumber thinly. Scrape, wash and grate the carrots. Halve the pepper, remove the pith and seeds, and cut into strips. Peel the onion and cut into rings. Clean, wash and drain the lamb's lettuce and radicchio. Tear the radicchio into large pieces. Halve the olives. Peel the cooked celeriac and slice with a stainless steel knife. Drain the cauliflower florets. • Arrange all the salad ingredients in sections on a large serving plate, and sprinkle with pepper. Arrange the olives on top. • Combine the oil, vinegar, salt, herbs and yogurt and pour this sauce over the salad. • Shell the egg, cut it into eight wedges, and use to garnish the salad.

Wild Herb Salad with Croûtons

For those who enjoy gathering and eating wild plants

200g/7oz mixed wild herbs, e.g. young dandelion leaves, sorrel, dead nettle leaves, ribwort, plantain leaves

1 lettuce (150g/5^{1}/$_{2}$oz)

1 small apple

1 tsp maple syrup

1 tsp lemon juice

3 tbsps walnut oil

1 tbsp apple vinegar

1 tbsp apple juice

^{1}/$_{4}$ tsp salt

2 tbsps chopped chives

2 slices wholewheat bread

1 clove garlic

2 tbsps vegetable margarine

Preparation time: 30 minutes
Nutritional value:
Analysis per serving, approx:
• 670kJ/160kcal
• 3g protein
• 8g fat
• 19g carbohydrate

Wash the wild herbs thoroughly, removing any long stems, and drain. Break the lettuce into leaves, wash well, and drain. Tear larger leaves into several pieces. Roughly chop the drained herbs, and mix them with the lettuce in a bowl. • Quarter, peel and core the apple, then cut into thin sticks. Mix these with the syrup, lemon juice, oil, vinegar, apple juice and salt. Toss the salad and the chives in this sauce. • Cut the bread into 1cm/^{1}/$_{2}$-inch cubes. Peel and crush the garlic. Mix the crushed garlic into the margarine, melt in a frying-pan, and fry the cubes of bread until golden. • Scatter these croûtons over the salad.

Spinach Salad with Orange

Ginger syrup is the liquid from a jar of stem ginger

400g/14oz very young spinach leaves

2 untreated oranges

1 apple

1 tbsp walnut oil

^{1}/$_{4}$ tsp salt

^{1}/$_{2}$ tsp ginger syrup

1 pot natural yogurt (150g/5^{1}/$_{2}$oz)

4 tbsps coarsely grated Jerusalem artichoke

Preparation time: 20 minutes
Nutritional value:
Analysis per serving, approx:
• 545kJ/130kcal
• 5g protein
• 4g fat
• 19g carbohydrate

Pick over the spinach leaves, wash and shake dry; remove the long stems and cut larger leaves in half. Peel 1 orange, and cut it into segments, removing any pips. Remove a thin layer of peel from the second orange, and cut into julienne strips. Squeeze out the juice. Peel, core and quarter the apple, and thinly slice the quarters. Put the spinach, orange and apple in a salad bowl. • Mix the orange juice, oil, salt, ginger syrup and yogurt together, and toss the salad ingredients in this sauce. Scatter the Jerusalem artichoke and strips of orange peel over the salad.

Our Tip: If Jerusalem artichoke is not available, cut two pieces of stem ginger into tiny pieces and scatter them over the salad. If you do not like orange peel, substitute coarsely chopped walnuts.

Asparagus Salad

Make only with fresh asparagus

500g/1lb 2oz asparagus
3l/4¹/₄ pints water
¹/₂ tsp salt
¹/₂ tsp sugar
3 tomatoes
3 hard-boiled eggs
4 tbsps corn oil
2 tbsps cider vinegar
¹/₂ tsp salt
A pinch of white pepper
2 tbsps chopped parsley

Preparation time: 10 minutes
Cooking time: 20-30 minutes
Standing time: 20 minutes

Nutritional value:
Analysis per serving, approx:
• 860kJ/205kcal
• 9g protein
• 15g fat
• 8g carbohydrate

Thinly peel the asparagus from top to bottom, cut off the woody ends and use kitchen string to tie the stems of asparagus into two bundles.Bring the water to the boil, adding the salt and sugar. Lay the bundles of asparagus in it, and cook, covered, over a low heat for 20-30 minutes depending on the thickness of the spears. • Pour boiling water over the tomatoes, peel and quarter, discarding the hard stalk ends. Finely dice the quartered tomatoes. • Lift the asparagus out of the water, rinse in cold water and drain on a tea-towel. Remove the string and cut the asparagus into pieces about 5cm/2 inches long. Shell the eggs and cut into eight wedges. Arrange the pieces of asparagus, the segments of egg and the diced tomato on a serving plate. • Mix the oil, vinegar, salt and pepper together and spoon this over the salad. • Cover the salad and refrigerate for 20 minutes for the flavours to combine. • Sprinkle chopped parsley over the salad before serving.

Salade Niçoise

One of the many variations of this classic French recipe

1 small lettuce
500g/1lb 2oz tomatoes
1 large onion
200g/7oz canned tuna
12 black olives, pitted
3 tbsps olive oil
1¹/₂ tbsps wine vinegar
¹/₂ tsp salt
¹/₄ tsp white pepper
1 tbsp fresh chopped basil
2 hard-boiled eggs

Preparation time: 20 minutes
Nutritional value:
Analysis per serving, approx:
• 1240kJ/295kcal
• 18g protein
• 22g fat
• 6g carbohydrate

Remove the outer lettuce leaves. Separate the lettuce into leaves, discarding any large stalks, wash, carefully pat dry and tear roughly into smaller pieces. • Wash and dry the tomatoes and cut into eight, removing the hard stalk ends. Peel the onion and slice into thin rings. Break the tuna into 3cm/1¹/₄-in pieces, and drain off the oil. Mix the tomato pieces, the onion rings, tuna, lettuce leaves and olives. • Mix the olive oil, vinegar, salt and pepper together, and spoon this sauce over the salad. • Sprinkle with the chopped basil. Shell the eggs, divide into eight segments and use to garnish the salad.

Our Tip: The basil may be replaced with dried mixed herbs.

A Selection of Bean Salads

The more tender the beans, the more elegant the salad

Wax Bean Salad
Illustrated in the background

500g/1lb 2oz wax beans
2 sprigs savory
100g/4oz shelled peas
2 egg yolks
2 tbsps cider vinegar
2 tsps mild mustard
Salt and white pepper
1 tsp concentrated apple juice
4 tbsps corn oil

Preparation time: 10 minutes
Cooking time: 15 minutes
Nutritional value:
Analysis per serving, approx:
• 735kJ/175kcal • 5g protein
• 12g fat • 11g carbohydrate

Wash the beans and top and tail them. Place them in a saucepan and cover them with water. Add salt and the savory and boil for about 15 minutes or until tender. • Cook the peas in a separate saucepan in a small amount of salted water for 5-10 minutes over gentle heat, then drain. • Mix the egg yolks, vinegar, mustard, salt, pepper, concentrated apple juice and oil together to make a dressing. • Drain the beans, and while still lukewarm mix with the peas. Pour the dressing over them.

French Bean Salad
Illustrated left in foreground

500g/1lb 2oz French beans
2 sprigs savory
Salt
2 spring onions
2 hard-boiled eggs
100g/4oz canned sweetcorn
2 tbsps sherry vinegar
4 tbsps olive oil
2 tbsps finely chopped dill

Preparation time: 10 minutes
Cooking time: 10 minutes

Nutritional value:
Analysis per serving, approx:
• 905kJ/215kcal • 7g protein
• 14g fat • 15g carbohydrate

Wash the beans and top and tail them. Place them in a saucepan and cover them with water. Add salt and the savory. Return to the boil and cook for 10 minutes. Drain and leave to cool. • Trim the spring onions, wash and slice finely. Shell the eggs and cut them into eight wedges. Drain the sweetcorn. • Combine the vinegar with salt and oil and mix with the sweetcorn and beans. • Arrange the pieces of egg on the salad and sprinkle with the dill.

Broad Bean Salad
Illustrated on the right

1kg/2¼lbs broad beans
2 sprigs savory
2 cloves garlic
2 tbsps cider vinegar
Salt and white pepper
5 tbsps walnut oil
5 fresh mint leaves

Preparation time: 10 minutes
Cooking time: 25 minutes
Standing time: 1 hour
Nutritional value:
Analysis per serving, approx:
• 1195kJ/285kcal
• 12g protein
• 13g fat
• 30g carbohydrate

Shell the broad beans. Cover them with boiling water and add salt and the savory. Return to the boil and cook for about 25 minutes. • Drain the beans and leave to cool. Peel the garlic and chop finely. • Combine the vinegar with salt, garlic, pepper and oil, and shred the mint leaves. Mix the dressing and mint with the beans. • Cover the salad and leave for an hour to allow the flavours to combine.

Cucumber Salad with Yogurt Dressing

A low-calorie salad to help the slimmer

Pepper Salad with Feta Cheese

Colourful, tasty and full of vitamins. You can use pecorino cheese instead of feta

| 1 large cucumber (about 1kg/2¹/₄lbs) |
| 1 pot natural yogurt (150g/5¹/₂oz) |
| ¹/₂ tsp salt |
| Pinch of white pepper |
| 1 tbsp lemon juice |
| 2 tsps maple or golden syrup |
| ¹/₂ punnet cress |

Preparation time: 10 minutes
Nutritional value:

Analysis per serving, approx:
- 355kJ/85kcal
- 3g protein
- 4g fat
- 9g carbohydrate

Wash and dry the cucumber, and halve lengthways; cut the halves in 5mm/¹/₄-inch slices. • Combine the yogurt with the salt, pepper, lemon juice and syrup and mix with the sliced cucumber. • Cut the cress with kitchen scissors, rinse in cold water, drain well, and pat dry. Sprinkle over the salad.

Our Tip: To alter the flavour of Cucumber Salad put 1 piece of chopped stem ginger and 1 tsp ginger syrup in the yogurt sauce in place of the maple syrup. Then scatter chopped fresh dill over the salad instead of cress. If a sweet-and-sour flavour is not desired, season the yogurt with salt, pepper, paprika and a little finely-chopped rosemary. Sprinkle freshly chopped borage over the salad. The salad will be creamier if crème fraîche is used instead of yogurt.

| 3 peppers, 1 green, 1 red, 1 yellow |
| 1 large onion |
| 100g/3¹/₂oz feta cheese |
| 1 large clove garlic |
| ¹/₂ tsp medium-hot mustard |
| Good pinch each of salt, white pepper and sugar |
| 1 tbsp cider vinegar |
| 3 tbsps olive oil |
| 2 tbsps chopped parsley |

Preparation time: 10 minutes
Nutritional value:

Analysis per serving, approx:
- 965kJ/230kcal
- 9g protein
- 16g fat
- 13g carbohydrate

Halve the peppers, remove the pith and seeds, wash, dry and cut into strips. Peel and chop the onion. Cut the cheese into small cubes. • Peel and finely chop the garlic, and mix with the mustard, salt, pepper, sugar, vinegar and oil. • Toss the peppers, onion and cheese in the vinaigrette dressing. • Serve the salad sprinkled with the chopped parsley.

Our Tip: The flavour of Pepper Salad may be altered by replacing the red pepper with 2 medium-sized tomatoes, peeled and diced, which are mixed in with the strips of pepper. Instead of the cheese use 200g/7oz cooked, diced chicken.

Potato Salads with a Difference

Try one of these salads for a spicy treat

New Potato Salad
Illustrated on the left

800g/1³/₄lbs small new potatoes
200g/7oz pickled herring fillets in cream
4 gherkins
2 shallots
1 tbsp cider vinegar
1 tsp lemon juice
¹/₂ tsp salt
¹/₂ tsp concentrated apple juice
1 tbsp walnut oil
2 hard-boiled eggs

Preparation time: 20 minutes
Cooking time: 12-15 minutes
Nutritional value:
Analysis per serving, approx:
• 1325kJ/315kcal
• 14g protein
• 13g fat
• 35g carbohydrate

Scrub the potatoes under cold running water, and cook them in their skins for 12-15 minutes, depending on their size. • Drain, leave to cool, peel and slice. • Cut the herrings into strips about 2cm/¹/₂ inch across, and finely dice the gherkins. Peel and chop the shallots. Combine the potatoes, gherkins, shallots, herrings and the cream sauce. • Make a dressing with the vinegar, lemon juice, salt, concentrated apple juice and oil. Mix this dressing into the salad. • Shell the eggs, cut them into eight wedges and use for garnish.

Potato Salad with Cucumber
Illustrated on the right

600g/1lb 6oz waxy potatoes
¹/₂ cucumber (about 400g/14oz)
1 apple
1 large onion
1 tsp salt
2 tbsps lemon juice
3 tsps maple or golden syrup
5 tbsps crème fraîche
3 tbsps chopped chives

Preparation time: 20 minutes
Cooking time: 25-30 minutes
Nutritional value:
Analysis per serving, approx:
• 860kJ/205kcal
• 5g protein
• 56g fat
• 35g carbohydrate

Scrub the potatoes under cold running water and cook them in their skins for 25-30 minutes, depending on their size. • Drain, leave to cool, then peel and slice them. Wash and dry the cucumber, and slice thinly. Peel the apple, cut in eight, remove the core, and cut the pieces into thin slices. Peel and chop the onion. • Mix all the salad ingredients with the salt, lemon juice, maple syrup and crème fraîche. • Serve the salad sprinkled with the chives.

Our Tip: Too strong an onion flavour can detract from the sweet-and-sour flavour. Try and use Spanish onions which are milder in flavour, or put the chopped onion in a sieve and run cold water over it for a milder flavour.

Salads for Colder Weather

Ringing the changes in the winter months

Chicory and Orange Salad
Illustrated on the left

4 medium-sized heads of chicory

1 orange

2 hard-boiled eggs

6 tbsps natural yogurt

2 tbsps crème fraîche

1/4 tsp each salt and sweet paprika

6 tbsps cress

Preparation time: 15 minutes
Nutritional value:
Analysis per serving, approx:
- 460kJ/110kcal
- 8g protein
- 5g fat
- 9g carbohydrate

Remove the outer leaves of the chicory, wash and dry the heads, and cut into 1cm/1/2-inch strips. Peel the orange, divide into segments removing the skin and any pips. Shell and chop the eggs.

• Mix the yogurt with the crème fraîche, salt and paprika, and combine this dressing, the diced eggs and orange segments with the chicory. • Scatter the cress leaves over the salad before serving.

Cauliflower salad
Illustrated in the front

1 small cauliflower

125ml/4 fl oz each milk and water

3 tbsps cider or raspberry vinegar

1/2 tsp seasoned salt

1/4 tsp white pepper

1 tsp honey

1/2 tsp mild mustard

4 tbsps grapeseed oil

1 tbsp celery leaves, chopped

2 tbsps parsley, chopped

Preparation time: 20 minutes
Cooking time: 12 minutes

Nutritional value:
Analysis per serving, approx:
- 800kJ/190kcal
- 7g protein
- 13g fat
- 12g carbohydrate

Remove the outer green leaves of the cauliflower, soak the head, florets downwards, in cold water for 10 minutes to flush out any dirt and insects, then break into florets and trim the stems. Bring the milk and water to the boil. Add the cauliflower and cook for 12 minutes. Drain and leave to cool. • Combine the vinegar, seasoned salt, pepper, honey and mustard. Add the oil and toss the cauliflower florets in this dressing. Cover and leave for about 30 minutes for the flavours to combine. • Serve the Cauliflower Salad sprinkled with the chopped celery leaves and parsley.

Celery Salad
Illustrated at the back

500g/1lb 2oz celery

1 fairly large red apple

1 tbsp lemon juice

1 tsp mild mustard • 1/2 tsp salt

1 tsp ginger syrup

125ml/4 fl oz whipping cream

Preparation time: 15 minutes
Nutritional value:
Analysis per serving, approx:
- 630kJ/150kcal • 2g protein
- 10g fat • 13g carbohydrate

Remove the celery leaves, chop and reserve. Slice the celery stalks. Cut the apple in eighths, remove the core, and slice each section thinly. • Combine the lemon juice, mustard, salt and syrup, and toss the sliced apple and celery in this dressing. Beat the cream until it begins to thicken, and fold into the salad. • Garnish with the celery leaves,

Raw Carrot and Apple Salad

Makes a slimming but filling supper eaten with wholewheat bread

Raw Carrot and Leek Salad

Low in calories, rich in vitamins

600g/1lb 6oz carrots
2 large apples
50g/2oz shelled walnuts
1 pot natural yogurt (150g/5¹/₂oz)
2 tbsps lemon juice
2 tsps unsweetened apple juice
¹/₄ tsp salt

Preparation time: 30 minutes
Standing time: 30 minutes
Nutritional value:
Analysis per serving, approx:
• 985kJ/235kcal
• 5g protein
• 10g fat
• 33g carbohydrate

Scrape, wash and coarsely grate the carrots. Quarter and core the apples; peel them and grate coarsely. Combine the grated carrot and apple in a bowl. Chop the walnuts coarsely, reserving 2 halves for garnish. • Stir the lemon juice, concentrated apple juice and salt into the yogurt, and mix this dressing and the chopped nuts into the salad. Cover, and refrigerate for about 30 minutes to allow the flavours to combine. • Serve garnished with the whole walnut halves.

Our Tip: For a richer salad, use cream or crème fraîche instead of yogurt. Add variety by adding 1 or 2 finely sliced stalks of celery to the carrot and apple.

300g/10oz leeks
400g/14oz carrots
1 large cooking apple
1 punnet cress
1 tbsp lemon juice
2 tbsps freshly chopped herbs, e.g. parsley, salad burnet, chives, lemon balm
125ml/4 fl oz thick-set natural yogurt
¹/₄ tsp salt
¹/₂ tsp concentrated pear juice

Preparation time: 20 minutes
Nutritional value:
Analysis per serving, approx:
• 545kJ/130kcal
• 4g protein
• 4g fat
• 19g carbohydrate

Trim the dark green tops and the roots from the leeks. Slit lengthways, wash thoroughly, pat dry and slice thinly. Scrape and wash the carrots, and slice them into julienne strips. Peel, quarter and core the apple, and grate coarsely. Cut the cress with kitchen scissors, place in a colander, rinse in cold water and drain well. • Arrange the leek, carrot and apple on a serving dish and sprinkle with the lemon juice. • Mix the herbs into the sour cream with the salt and concentrated pear juice and pour this over the salad. • Garnish with little bunches of cress.

Our Tip: To serve this as a light evening meal, strips of cooked chicken may be mixed in with the vegetables. If the flavour of the cress is too strong, substitute a handful of lamb's lettuce (corn salad).

Avocado Salad

Rich in vitamins, tasty and wholesome

2 avocados
1 red pepper
1 stick celery
1/2 onion
4 gherkins
100g/4oz low-fat curd cheese
1 egg yolk
2 tbsps corn oil
1 tbsp lemon juice
1 tsp mustard
Dash of Worcestershire sauce
1 tsp salt
1/4 tsp white pepper
2 tbsps small capers, rinsed and drained

Preparation time: 10 minutes
Nutritional value:
Analysis per serving, approx:
- 1220kJ/290kcal
- 7g protein
- 25g fat
- 9g carbohydrate

Quarter the avocados. Remove the stones, peel, and cut into thin slices. Halve the pepper, remove the pith and seeds; wash, dry and chop the pepper halves. Wash the celery and cut into thin slices. Peel and dice the onion. Chop the gherkins. • Mix the curd cheese with the egg yolk, oil, lemon juice, mustard, Worcestershire sauce, salt, pepper and capers. • Mix the sliced avocado, diced pepper, sliced celery, diced onion and gherkins with the dressing.

Our Tip: This recipe requires forward planning. The avocados must be completely ripe. Only fully ripe fruit have the characteristic, subtle avocado taste. Unripe avocados will ripen if kept in a paper bag and left in an airing cupboard for 2-3 days.

Raw Beetroot Salad

Do not use pre-cooked beetroot

Grated Celeriac with Pineapple

Also makes a good starter

600g/1lb 6oz small beetroot
2 large apples
2 small onions
2 tbsps lemon juice
1 tbsp golden syrup
Pinch each of salt, white pepper, and ground caraway seed
2 tbsps walnut or grapeseed oil

Preparation time: 20 minutes
Nutritional value:
Analysis per serving, approx:
• 800kJ/190kcal
• 3g protein
• 6g fat
• 31g carbohydrate

Scrub the beetroots thoroughly under running lukewarm water, peel and slice them finely. Then cut the slices into julienne strips. Put these in a salad bowl. Peel the apples, cut into eighths, remove the core and cut the sections into thin slices. Peel and finely chop the onions. • Mix the lemon juice, syrup, salt, pepper and caraway together, and combine this dressing, the onion and sliced apple into the beetroot salad. • Finally sprinkle with the walnut oil.

Our Tip: For a stronger flavour, add 100g/4oz grated raw turnip to the salad, and season the sauce with 1-2 tsps freshly grated horseradish or 1 tsp mustard powder.

500g/1lb 2oz celeriac
2 tbsps lemon juice
1 large cooking apple
2 slices fresh pineapple (about 1cm/½ inch thick - 200g/7oz)
Good pinch each of salt and white pepper
2 tsps maple or golden syrup
125ml/4 fl oz single cream
50g/2oz shelled walnuts

Preparation time: 20 minutes
Nutritional value:
Analysis per serving, approx:
• 1260kJ/300kcal
• 5g protein
• 19g fat
• 28g carbohydrate

Peel and wash the celeriac, cut into thin slices, and cut the slices into julienne strips. Sprinkle immediately with the lemon juice. Peel, quarter and core the apple, and cut into julienne strips. Mix the apple and celeriac together. Cut away the pineapple skin and cut the flesh into very thin segments. Mix these into the salad. • Combine the salt, pepper, maple syrup and cream, and toss the salad in this dressing. • Chop the walnuts finely, and scatter over the salad.

Our Tip: Celeriac is sometimes hard to find in Britain. Grated daikon (mooli) or turnip make a good substitute although the flavour will be very different.

Raw Mushroom Salad

Cultivated mushrooms taste delicious raw, especially those with brown caps

400g/14oz button mushrooms
200g/7oz fresh prawns
1 tbsp wine vinegar
1 tbsp lemon juice
3 tbsps walnut oil
$1/4$ tsp each salt and sugar
A pinch of white pepper
2 tbsps dry sherry
1 tbsp parsley, chopped
1 tbsp chives, chopped

Preparation time: 15 minutes
Standing time: 30 minutes
Nutritional value:
Analysis per serving, approx:
• 610kJ/145kcal
• 11g protein
• 11g fat
• 4g carbohydrate

Trim the mushrooms, wash, pat dry, and slice thinly. Briefly rinse the prawns, drain, and mix in a bowl with the mushrooms. • Combine the vinegar, lemon juice, oil, salt, sugar, pepper and sherry , and toss the salad in this dressing. • Cover, and refrigerate for 30 minutes to allow the flavours to mingle. • Scatter the herbs over the salad before serving.

Our Tip: Instead of prawns, use finely diced lean ham. For a milder sauce, replace the vinegar with pineapple or apple juice.

Raw Kohlrabi Salad

This is the best way to eat kohlrabi

2 large kohlrabi (about 700g/1lb 9oz)
2 tbsps lemon juice
1 stick celery
1 large cooking apple
1 pot natural yogurt (150g/5$1/2$oz)
Good pinch each of salt and white pepper
2 tsps blackstrap molasses or black treacle
1 tbsp chopped salad burnet

Preparation time: 10 minutes
Nutritional value:
Analysis per serving, approx:
• 485kJ/115kcal
• 6g protein
• 0.5g fat
• 23g carbohydrate

Peel, wash and dry the kohlrabi. Wash the heart-shaped green leaves, chop finely, cover and reserve. Coarsely grate the kohlrabi and mix with the lemon juice. Break off the celery stalk, wash the green leaves, chop finely and set aside with the kohlrabi leaves. Remove any coarse fibres from the celery, wash, dry and cut into thin slices. Peel the apple, cut in eighths, remove the core and cut the eighths into thin slices. Mix the celery and apple with the grated kohlrabi. • Stir the salt, pepper and molasses into the yogurt, and toss the raw vegetables in this sauce. Scatter the chopped leaves and salad burnet over the salad.

Our Tip: Cucumber may be substituted for the celery and apple. If so, cut the kohlrabi and cucumber into julienne strips, and replace the salad burnet with a generous sprinkling of chopped chives.

Different Ways of Serving Chinese Leaves

Their delicate flavour goes with almost anything

Chinese Leaves and Radish Salad
Illustrated on the left

600g/1lb 6oz Chinese leaves
3 bunches radishes
1 red pepper
1 small onion
4 tbsps grapefruit juice
3 tbsps safflower oil
1 tsp mild mustard
Generous pinch of salt
1/2 tsp ginger syrup
2 tbsps chopped chives

Preparation time: 15 minutes
Nutritional value:
Analysis per serving, approx:
- 525kJ/125kcal • 3g protein
- 8g fat • 10g carbohydrate

Discard the tough outer leaves of the Chinese leaves. Wash them thoroughly, shake dry, and shred. Trim the green parts from the radishes, wash well and slice very thinly. Halve the pepper, remove the pith and seeds, wash and chop finely. Peel the onion and chop finely. • Combine the grapefruit juice with the oil, mustard, salt and syrup. Toss the salad in this dressing, and scatter with chives.

Chinese Leaves with Gammon
Illustrated at the back

600g/1lb 6oz Chinese leaves
1 large onion
1/2 tsp salt
A pinch of black pepper
2 tsps concentrated pear juice
3 tbsps cider vinegar
2 tbsps apple juice
3 tbsps grapeseed oil
100g/4oz gammon
2 tbsps chopped fresh parsley

Preparation time: 20 minutes
Nutritional value:

Analysis per serving, approx:
- 945kJ/225kcal • 7g protein
- 17g fat • 10g carbohydrate

Prepare the Chinese leaves as for Chinese Leaves and Radish Salad, and shred them. Peel the onion and chop finely. • Mix the salt, pepper, concentrated pear juice, vinegar, apple juice and oil together, and toss the salad in this dressing. • Dice the gammon, fry in a dry frying-pan until the fat runs, and mix the diced gammon and fat into the salad. • Scatter with parsley before serving.

Chinese Leaves with Fresh Fruit
Illustrated at the front

600g/1lb 6oz Chinese leaves
2 kiwi fruit
2 oranges
3 tbsps crème fraîche
3 tbsps thick-set natural yogurt
1 tbsp lemon juice
Salt and pepper
4 tbsps chopped watercress

Preparation time: 20 minutes
Nutritional value:
Analysis per serving, approx:
- 335kJ/80kcal
- 3g protein
- 4g fat
- 9g carbohydrate

Prepare the Chinese leaves as for Chinese Leaves and Radish Salad, and shred them. Peel the kiwi fruit and the oranges. Cut the kiwi fruit into slices about 5mm/1/4-inch thick, then quarter each slice. Divide the orange into segments and remove the skin. • Combine the crème fraîche, yogurt, lemon juice, salt, pepper and chopped watercress. Mix dressing with the other salad ingredients.

White Cabbage Salad with Bacon

Can be prepared well in advance

Spicy Sauerkraut Salad

Ideal with cold cooked meats or frankfurters

1 small white cabbage (about 1kg/2¼lbs)
2l/3½ pints water
1 tsp salt
200g/7oz lean back bacon
1 tsp salt
2 tsps golden syrup
2 tsps crushed caraway seeds
Pinch of white pepper
2-3 tbsps wine vinegar
3 tbsps white wine
2 tbsps walnut oil

Preparation time: 30 minutes
Standing time: 1 hour
Nutritional value:
Analysis per serving, approx:
• 1805kJ/430kcal
• 8g protein
• 38g fat
• 13g carbohydrate

Discard the outer leaves of the cabbage. Cut in quarters, remove the stalk, and shred. Bring the salted water to the boil. Put the cabbage in a sieve or colander and blanch in the salted water for 4 minutes. Then drain. • Dice the bacon, and fry in a dry frying-pan until brown and crisp. • Combine the salt, syrup, caraway seeds, pepper and oil. • Toss the well-drained cabbage in this dressing. Pour the diced bacon with its fat onto the salad. • Cover and leave to stand at room temperature for 1 hour to allow the flavours to mingle.

Our Tip: Do not be surprised at the use of syrup. All syrups contain flavouring and nutrients as well as sweetness. Therefore in modern cookery they are a welcome, though still unusual, form of seasoning for many types of food.

800g/1¾lbs sauerkraut
1 large onion
1 large gherkin
3 slices fresh pineapple
125ml/4 fl oz pure pineapple juice
4 tbsps brine from the gherkins
2 tbsps safflower oil

Preparation time: 10 minutes
Standing time: 20 minutes
Nutritional value:
Analysis per serving, approx:
• 755kJ/180kcal
• 5g protein
• 6g fat
• 28g carbohydrate

Place the sauerkraut in a large bowl, and use two forks to loosen and separate it. Peel the onion and chop very finely. Finely dice the gherkin. Peel the pineapple, and dice it. • Mix the pineapple juice, brine and safflower oil together. Combine the diced onion and gherkin and pieces of pineapple with the sauerkraut and toss in the salad dressing. • Cover and leave for about 20 minutes at room temperature to allow the flavours to mingle.

Our Tip: If liked, 100g/4oz raisins can be added. For a stronger flavour, use 6 tbsps of the gherkin brine and add some cider vinegar to taste.

72

Red Cabbage and Fruit Salad

A real treat of raw fruit and vegetables

700g/1¹/₂lbs red cabbage
2l/3¹/₂ pints water
1 tsp salt
5 tbsps cider vinegar
1 tbsp lemon juice
2 tbsps concentrated pear juice
¹/₂ tsp salt
1 apple
1 large orange
1 banana
250g/8oz fresh pineapple slices
3 tbsps walnut or grapeseed oil

Preparation time: 30 minutes
Standing time: 30 minutes
Nutritional value:
Analysis per serving, approx:
• 1155kJ/275kcal
• 4g protein
• 8g fat
• 47g carbohydrate

Discard the outer leaves of the red cabbage. Cut in quarters, cut out a wedge from the main stalk, and shred the cabbage quarters. Bring the water to the boil with the salt and 3 tbsps cider vinegar. Put the shredded cabbage in a sieve or colander and blanch it in the boiling water for 4 minutes, then drain thoroughly. • Stir the lemon juice, remaining vinegar, concentrated pear juice and salt together. Mix this dressing into the cabbage in a large bowl, pressing it down a little. • Peel the apple, cut it into eighths, remove the core and cut the eighths into small slices. Peel the pineapple slices and cut into small pieces. Mix all the fruit and the oil into the red cabbage. • Cover the salad and leave at room temperature for 30 minutes to allow the flavours to mingle.

Brussels Sprout Salad with Jerusalem Artichoke

Makes a good evening meal

800g/1³/₄lbs Brussels sprouts
1 tsp salt
100g/4oz streaky bacon
2 shallots
50g/2oz Jerusalem artichoke
2 tbsps sunflower oil
2 tbsps white wine vinegar
6 tbsps vegetable stock
2 tbsps chopped parsley

Preparation time: 10 minutes
Cooking time: 20 minutes
Nutritional value:
Analysis per serving, approx:
• 1365kJ/325kcal
• 13g protein
• 23g fat
• 16g carbohydrate

Remove the outer leaves of the Brussels sprouts, and trim the stems. Wash, sprinkle with the salt and put in a saucepan. Add just enough water to cover and cook gently for up to about 20 minutes depending on size. Drain thoroughly in a colander. • Dice the bacon. Peel the shallots, and chop finely. Peel the Jerusalem artichoke, wash, grate, and set aside. • Heat the oil, sauté the diced bacon until crisp, then remove from the fat with a slotted spoon. Sauté the shallot in the remaining fat until golden. • Mix the wine vinegar, vegetable stock, shallots, frying fat and grated artichoke into the Brussels sprouts. Scatter the diced bacon and chopped parsley over the salad.

Light Broccoli Salad

Broccoli makes a delicious salad ingredient

Broccoli Salad with Turkey
Illustrated on the left

800g/1³/₄lbs broccoli
1 onion
200g/7oz turkey breast fillets
4 tbsps walnut oil
Salt and white pepper
2 tbsps white wine vinegar
1 small pot natural yogurt
8 shelled walnuts

Preparation time: 10 minutes
Cooking time: 12 minutes
Nutritional value:
Analysis per serving, approx:
• 1195kJ/285kcal • 5g protein
• 6g fat • 28g carbohydrate

Prepare the broccoli as described in the recipe for Broccoli Salad with Coconut, cook in salted water, drain and leave to cool. • Peel and chop the onion. Wash and dry the turkey, and cut the meat into 2cm/³/₄-inch cubes. • Heat 2 tbsps oil. Sauté the onion until golden. Add the diced turkey, and sauté for about 4 minutes. Season the meat with salt and pepper. • Mix the remaining oil with the white wine vinegar and yogurt, and fold into the broccoli with the onion and turkey. • Chop the walnuts coarsely and scatter over.

Broccoli Salad with Prawns
Illustrated in the foreground

200g/7oz large frozen prawns
800g/1³/₄lbs broccoli
1 large apple
Salt and white pepper
1 tsp sugar
2 tbsps lemon juice
3 tbsps peach nectar
4 tbsps safflower oil
2 tbsps chopped chives

Preparation time: 10 minutes
Cooking time: 12 minutes
Nutritional value:
Analysis per serving, approx:
• 1010kJ/240kcal • 16g protein
• 11g fat • 18g carbohydrate

Thaw the prawns in a covered container. • Prepare the broccoli as described in the following recipe, and cook in salted water. • Peel and core the apple, cut into julienne strips, and combine with salt, pepper, sugar, lemon juice, peach nectar and oil. • Fold the salad dressing and prawns into the broccoli.

Broccoli Salad with Coconut
Illustrated on the right

800g/1³/₄lbs broccoli
3 hard-boiled eggs
1 onion
Salt and white pepper
Dash of Tabasco sauce
4 tbsps orange juice
4 tbsps corn oil
50g/2oz shredded coconut

Preparation time: 15 minutes
Cooking time: 12 minutes
Nutritional value:
Analysis per serving, approx:
• 1240kJ/295kcal • 14g protein
• 22g fat • 14g carbohydrate

Trim and wash the broccoli and divide into florets. Cut off the stalks, peel and cut into evenly-sized pieces. Cover with boiling salted water and cook, for 6 minutes, then cover the pan with a lid and continue to cook until tender. • Drain the broccoli and leave to cool. Shell the eggs and chop finely. • Peel and grate the onion, and combine with the pepper, Tabasco sauce, orange juice and oil. Toss the broccoli in this dressing. • Sprinkle with the chopped egg and shredded coconut.

Leaf Spinach with Wild Herbs

The herbs used depend on what you can find

Swiss Chard in Cream Sauce

A subtle recipe for Swiss Chard

300g/10oz mixed wild herbs, such as greater plantain, coltsfoot, mallow, sorrel, chickweed, good king Henry and young dead nettle
500g/1lb 2oz very young spinach
4 l/7 pints water
2 tsps salt
1 large onion
2 cloves garlic
2 tbsps safflower oil
Pinch of salt
1 tsp honey
125ml/4 fl oz sour cream
50g/2oz pine kernels

Preparation time: 1 hour
Nutritional value:
Analysis per serving, approx:
• 1135kJ/270kcal
• 9g protein
• 16g fat
• 22g carbohydrate

Thoroughly wash the wild herbs and spinach leaves, discarding any coarse stems. • Bring the water to the boil, adding the salt. Blanch the herbs and spinach in the water for 3 minutes. • Then drain in a colander, and chop coarsely. Peel and finely chop the onion and garlic. • Heat the oil, and sauté the diced onion and garlic until transparent. Add the chopped vegetables, and cook, covered, over a low heat for 5 minutes. • Mix the salt, honey and sour cream into the vegetables. Leave the uncovered saucepan over a gentle heat for a few minutes to let some of the moisture evaporate. • Meanwhile, chop the pine kernels, and scatter them over the vegetables. • This salad tastes good with boiled potatoes and fried eggs, or nut roast or croquettes made with textured vegetable protein.

1kg/2¼lbs Swiss chard
250ml/8fl oz hot vegetable stock
2 tsps wholewheat flour
2 tbsps pure pineapple juice
Pinch each of salt and grated nutmeg
25g/1oz peanut butter
Few drops lemon juice
125ml/4 fl oz single cream

Preparation time: 20 minutes
Cooking time: 10 minutes
Nutritional value:
Analysis per serving, approx:
• 840kJ/200kcal
• 8g protein
• 14g fat
• 11g carbohydrate

Thoroughly wash the Swiss chard, stripping off a handful of the green leaves and setting them aside. Cover them. • Shred the remaining chard, add to the hot vegetable stock and cook gently in a covered saucepan over a low heat for 10 minutes. •Stir the flour into the pineapple juice. Use this to thicken the vegetable mixture. Season to taste with salt, nutmeg, peanut butter and lemon juice. Stir the cream into the vegetables. Leave the uncovered saucepan over a gentle heat to let some of the moisture evaporate. • Meanwhile, finely chop the reserved chard leaves and scatter them over the cooked vegetables. • Mashed potatoes and poached eggs or lamb chops make good accompaniments.

Gourmet Recipes for Garden Peas and Mange-tout

Special side dishes for festive occasions

Mange-tout Peas in Wine Sauce

Illustrated in the foreground

700g/1lb 9oz mange-tout peas
25g/1oz butter
125ml/4 fl oz hot vegetable stock
3 egg yolks
1 tbsp cornflour
Pinch each of salt and white pepper
125ml/4 fl oz dry white wine
Few drops lemon juice
1/4 tsp grated lemon rind
4 tbsps single cream
3 egg whites
2 tbsps finely chopped dill

Preparation time: 15 minutes
Cooking time: 10-15 minutes
Nutritional value:
Analysis per serving, approx:
• 905kJ/215kcal
• 11g protein
• 12g fat
• 15g carbohydrate

Wash the mange-tout peas, top and tail and dry thoroughly. • Melt the butter, and toss the mange-tout in it. Pour the vegetable stock over the peas, cover and cook gently for 10-15 minutes; drain off and reserve the cooking liquid. • Beat the egg yolks with the cornflour, salt and pepper, and heat in a double boiler, stirring constantly. Gradually stir in white wine, and adjust the flavour with the lemon juice and rind. Add the cream and cooking liquid to the sauce. • Beat the egg whites until stiff, and fold into the sauce. Mix the mange-tout with the sauce, and sprinkle the dill leaves over the whole dish. • A good accompaniment for turkey cutlets and mashed potato.

Peas and Pommes Duchesse

Illustrated in the background

800g/1³/₄lbs floury potatoes
2 tsps salt
500g/1lb 2oz young peas, shelled
125-250ml/4-8 fl oz vegetable stock
1/4 tsp sugar
50g/2oz butter
2 egg yolks
Pinch each of white pepper and grated nutmeg
1 egg yolk • 2 tbsps milk
4 tbsps freshly grated cheese
25g/1oz butter
Oil for the baking sheet

Preparation time: 30 minutes
Cooking time: 35-40 minutes
Nutritional value:
Analysis per serving, approx:
• 1595kJ/380kcal • 15g protein
• 15g fat • 46g carbohydrate

Peel, wash and dice the potatoes and boil, covered, in salted water for up to 25 minutes until tender. • Gently braise the peas in the vegetable stock with 1/2 tsp salt and the sugar in a covered saucepan. • Drain the cooked potatoes, allow to cool and push through a vegetable mill. • Preheat the oven to 200°C/400°F/Gas Mark 6. Grease a baking sheet with oil. • Combine the puréed potato with 1/2 tsp salt, the butter, egg yolks, pepper and nutmeg. Using a forcing bag, pipe the potato mixture into 8 equal portions on the baking sheet, hollowing out each to make a nest. Beat the egg yolk and milk together, and use to glaze the potato. • Drain the peas, and fill the potato nests. Sprinkle each with cheese, and dot with dabs of butter. • Cook on the middle shelf of the oven for 10-15 minutes.

Ideas Using Fresh Beans

The flavour of beans is improved by subtle seasoning

Broad Beans in Béchamel Sauce

Illustrated in the background

1¹/₂kg/3lbs 6oz broad beans (fresh or frozen)

500ml/16 fl oz vegetable stock

2 sprigs savory

25g/1oz butter

1 tbsp flour

1 small onion

¹/₂ bay leaf

2 cloves

Pinch each of salt, pepper and grated nutmeg

125ml/4 fl oz single cream

1 tsp anchovy paste

2 tbsps chopped parsley

Preparation time: 15 minutes
Cooking time: 1 hour
Nutritional value:
Analysis per serving, approx:
• 1220kJ/290kcal
• 12g protein
• 15g fat
• 26g carbohydrate

Shell the beans, rinse in cold water and drain. Bring the vegetable stock to the boil with the savory. Add the beans, and cook, covered, for 30 minutes. • Drain the beans, reserving 375ml/³/₄pint of the cooking liquid. • Melt the butter. Sprinkle in the flour, and stir until pale yellow, then gradually add the cooking liquid. • Peel the onion, stick the bay leaf and cloves into it, and place it in the sauce. Let the sauce simmer for 30 minutes, stirring frequently. • Remove the onion, and season to taste with salt, pepper and nutmeg. Combine the cream and anchovy paste, then mix into the sauce. Lastly add the broad beans to the sauce. • Serve sprinkled with parsley.

Green Beans with Crème Fraîche

Illustrated in the foreground

800g/1³/₄lbs French or runner beans

1 onion

1 clove garlic

2 medium-sized carrots

2 tbsps corn oil

125ml/4 fl oz hot vegetable stock

2 sprigs savory

1 tsp arrowroot

4 tbsps crème fraîche

2 tsps chopped fresh thyme or 1 tsp dried thyme

Preparation time: 20 minutes
Cooking time: 10-20 minutes
Nutritional value:
Analysis per serving, approx:
• 775kJ/185kcal
• 7g protein
• 10g fat
• 19g carbohydrate

Top and tail the beans, stringing them if necessary, and wash. Halve or quarter large beans. Peel and chop the onion and garlic very finely. Scrape, wash and finely dice the carrots. • Heat the oil and sauté the onion and garlic in it. Add the beans and diced carrot and quickly toss in the fat. Top up with the vegetable stock, and add the savory. Cook for 10-20 minutes depending on the thickness of the beans. • Dissolve the arrowroot in 1 tbsp cold water, and mix with the crème fraîche. Use this to thicken the sauce. Remove the savory. Sprinkle the thyme over the vegetables. • Green Beans with Crème Fraîche makes a good accompaniment for lamb chops and jacket potatoes.

Aubergines with Tomato Sauce

The taste of southern summers

1kg/2¼lbs small aubergines

2 tsps salt

1 onion

2 cloves garlic

6 tomatoes

4 tbsps wholewheat flour

125ml/4 fl oz olive oil

1 tsp chopped rosemary

Pinch each of salt and white pepper

1 tsp wholewheat flour

1 tbsp cider vinegar

Preparation time including standing time: 40 minutes
Cooking time: 35 minutes
Nutritional value:
Analysis per serving, approx:
• 1785kJ/420kcal
• 7g protein
• 32g fat
• 26g carbohydrate

Peel the aubergines, slice lengthways in 1cm/½-in slices, sprinkle with salt, cover and leave for 30 minutes to allow the bitter juices to run. • Peel and chop the onion and garlic. Removing the stalk ends from the tomatoes, skin them and cut in eight sections. • Drain the aubergines, pat dry and coat with flour. • Heat the oil. Fry the aubergine slices a few at a time until golden brown on both sides, drain on absorbent paper, and keep in a warm place. • Discard half the oil. Fry the diced onion and garlic in the remaining oil until golden. Add the tomatoes and cook for a further 2 minutes. Add the rosemary, salt and pepper, cover, and cook gently for another 5 minutes. • Stir the flour into the vinegar, being careful to remove all lumps and use to thicken the tomato sauce; simmer gently for another 5 minutes. • Boiled rice, sliced polenta or grilled meat are good with this dish.

Braised Courgettes

A good accompaniment for gammon

800g/1¾lbs small courgettes

2 cloves garlic

1 tsp salt

¼ tsp black pepper

100g/4oz streaky bacon

2 tbsps olive oil

125ml/4 fl oz hot vegetable stock

1 tbsp chopped fresh sage or 1 tsp dried sage

6 tbsps single cream

Pinch of hot paprika

2 tbsps chopped chives

Preparation time: 30 minutes
Cooking time: 20 minutes
Nutritional value:
Analysis per serving, approx:
• 1365kJ/325kcal
• 6g protein
• 27g fat
• 14g carbohydrate

Wash and dry the courgettes, remove the stalk ends and cut into 2cm/¾-inch cubes. Peel and chop the garlic, and crush with the salt and pepper. Mix the courgettes in a bowl with the garlic. • Dice the bacon, fry in the oil and remove, using a slotted spoon. • Sauté the diced courgettes in the oil, browning on all sides. Add the vegetable stock and sage and braise, covered, over a gentle heat for 15 minutes. • Combine the paprika and the cream, mix into the courgettes, and continue cooking, uncovered, over a low heat to reduce the liquid. • Serve the courgettes sprinkled with the diced bacon and chopped chives. • This goes well with potato croquettes.

Our Tip: Use diced lean ham or 200g/7oz diced cooked chicken instead of the bacon. This would reduce the calorie count by about 420kJ/110kcal.

Carrots – the Vegetable Top of the Pops!

Carrots taste best with mild seasoning

Glazed Carrots
In the background

800g/1³/₄lbs carrots
3 tbsps grapeseed oil
1 tbsp maple or golden syrup
125ml/4 fl oz vegetable stock
2 tsps arrowroot
3 tbsps single cream
Pinch of salt
1 tbsp chopped mint

Preparation time: 20 minutes
Cooking time: 20 minutes
Nutritional value:
Analysis per serving, approx:
- 775kJ/185kcal
- 4g protein
- 10g fat • 20g carbohydrate

Scrub the carrots thoroughly under cold running water, and cut into 1cm/¹/₂-inch cubes. • Heat the oil. Add the syrup, and fry the diced carrots in this mixture for 5 minutes, stirring frequently. Pour this over the vegetable stock. Cook gently, covered, over a low heat for 20 minutes; add a little more stock if required. • Stir the arrowroot into the cream. Use this to thicken the liquid in which the carrots have been cooked. Add salt, and sprinkle with the mint.

Carrots in Marsala
In the foreground

800g/1³/₄lbs carrots
45g/1¹/₂oz butter
125ml/4 fl oz Marsala
¹/₂ tsp salt
2 tbsps chopped parsley

Preparation time: 10 minutes
Cooking time: 20-30 minutes
Nutritional value:
Analysis per serving, approx:
- 755kJ/180kcal
- 2g protein
- 7g fat • 22g carbohydrate

Scrape, wash and slice the carrots. • Sauté them in the melted butter for 5 minutes. Add the Marsala and salt, and mix thoroughly. • Cover, and cook for 20-30 minutes or until tender. • Scatter parsley over the carrots.

Vegetables au Gratin

One of the best ways of serving delicate vegetables

Fennel with a Cheese Topping
Illustrated in foreground

800g/1³/₄lbs fennel	
50g/2oz butter	
2 tbsps flour	
125ml/4 fl oz warm milk	
Pinch each of salt, white pepper and grated nutmeg	
4 tbsps freshly grated Parmesan	

Preparation time: 20 minutes
Cooking time: 50 minutes
Nutritional value:
Analysis per serving, approx:
- 1115kJ/265kcal
- 10g protein
- 15g fat
- 22g carbohydrate

Trim, wash and quarter the fennel bulbs. Finely chop the green leaves and reserve. • Cook the fennel in salted water to cover for 40 minutes in a covered saucepan. • Butter an ovenproof dish. Preheat the oven to 220°C/430°F/Gas Mark 7. • Drain the fennel, reserving 125ml/4 fl oz of the cooking liquid. Melt 25g/1oz butter. Sprinkle with the flour, stir until pale yellow, then stir in the measured cooking liquid. Add the milk, and cook for a few minutes, stirring constantly; season to taste with the salt, pepper and nutmeg. • Place the fennel in the ovenproof dish, cover with the sauce and the chopped fennel leaves. Sprinkle with the cheese, and dot with the rest of the butter. Cook, uncovered, in the oven for 10 minutes.

A variation on the above:
Celery with a Cheese Topping
Illustrated in background

Trim 1kg/2¹/₂lbs celery, cut into 6cm/2¹/₂-inch lengths, and cook in salted water in a covered saucepan for 30 minutes. Chop the green celery leaves. • Place the celery in an ovenproof dish, pour the béchamel sauce over it and bake as described above for fennel. Sprinkle with the chopped celery leaves before serving.

Sweet-and-sour Cooked Cucumber

Creamy. light and easily digestible

1kg/2¼lbs cucumbers, preferably ridge
2 tbsps vegetable margarine
1 tsp mild mustard
½ tsp salt
1 tsp maple or golden syrup
1-2 tbsps lemon juice
125ml/4 fl oz vegetable stock
1 egg yolk
6 tbsps single cream
2 tbsps finely chopped dill

Preparation time: 15 minutes
Cooking time: 20 minutes
Nutritional value:
Analysis per serving, approx:
• 590kJ/140kcal
• 3g protein
• 11g fat
• 7g carbohydrate

Peel the cucumbers and cut them in half lengthways. Scrape out the seeds and cut into 5mm/¼-inch slices. • Melt the margarine and sauté the cucumber in it. Stir the mustard, salt, syrup and lemon juice into the mixture. Add the vegetable stock and braise, covered, over a low heat for 20 minutes. • Remove the lid from the saucepan and leave over a low heat for a few minutes to allow some of the liquid to evaporate, then remove from the heat and allow to cool slightly. • Beat the egg yolk and the cream together. Incorporate 2 tbsps of the hot braising liquid into this mixture and return gradually to the sauce. Adjust the seasoning to give a powerful sweet-and-sour flavour, and serve sprinkled with the chopped dill. • Mashed potatoes and vegeburgers make good accompaniments.

Our Tip: For a thicker sauce, mix 1-2 tsps cornflour dissolved in cold water with the vegetables before adding the cream, bring briefly to the boil, and then add with the egg yolk and cream.

Turnips in Rich Sauce

Turnips are both delicious and economical

800g/1¾lbs white turnips
1 tsp salt
25g/1oz butter
2 tbsps flour
1 tbsp butter
2 tbsps sugar
3 tbsps port

Preparation time: 30 minutes
Cooking time: 20 minutes
Nutritional value:
Analysis per serving, approx:
• 610kJ/145kcal
• 2g protein
• 7g fat
• 17g carbohydrate

Peel the turnips, wash thoroughly, dry and cut into small cubes. Cover with salted water, bring to the boil, and cook for about 20 minutes. • Drain in a colander, reserving the water; measure out 500ml/16 fl oz and reserve. • Melt the butter in a large saucepan. Sprinkle with the flour, and cook, stirring constantly, until pale yellow. Gradually add the vegetable water; beat vigorously with a whisk, and cook for a few minutes. • Add the turnip to the sauce • Then heat the butter in a small saucepan. Add the sugar, and cook until caramelized, stirring all the time. Stir in the port and add this sauce to the turnips, mixing thoroughly. • Simmer over a very low heat for another 5 minutes. • This tastes good with parsley potatoes and pork cutlets.

Our Tip: Try white turnips in béchamel sauce, made with half milk and half vegetable water, and seasoned with salt, a pinch of white pepper and nutmeg. Instead of the caramel sauce add 3-4 tbsps chopped chives

81

Cauliflower in Cream Sauce

Do not overcook cauliflower – it should still be crisp

1kg/2¼lbs cauliflower

500ml/16 fl oz milk

500ml/16 fl oz water

45g/1½oz vegetable margarine

1 tbsp wholewheat flour

125ml/4 fl oz single cream

2 egg yolks

½ tsp salt

Pinch of grated nutmeg

2 tbsps chopped chives

Preparation time: 35 minutes
Cooking time: 30-35 minutes
Nutritional value:
Analysis per serving, approx:
• 1070kJ/255kcal
• 9g protein
• 18g fat • 14g carbohydrate

Discard the outer leaves of the cauliflower, trim the stalk, and make a crosswise incision in the bottom; this allows the centre to cook as quickly as the more tender florets. Soak the cauliflower head, florets downwards, in cold water for 15 minutes to remove any dirt or insects. • Combine the water and milk and bring to the boil. Cook the cauliflower, florets uppermost, in a covered saucepan for 20-25 minutes or until tender. • Then drain the cauliflower, reserving 250ml/9 fl oz of the cooking liquid, divide into florets and keep warm. • Melt the margarine. Stir in the flour and cook, stirring constantly, until pale yellow, then gradually stir in the measured cooking liquid. Continue cooking the sauce gently for 10 minutes, stirring all the time. • Beat the cream, egg yolks, salt and nutmeg together, and incorporate into 2 tbsps of the hot sauce. Remove the sauce from the heat, and stir in the egg-and-cream mixture. Return the cauliflower florets to the sauce and reheat the entire dish, but do not let it boil. • Before serving, sprinkle the chopped chives over the cauliflower. • This dish goes well with mashed potatoes and grilled tomatoes.

Glazed Sweet Potatoes

This is a favourite dish from the Deep South of the United States

800g/1¾lbs yellow sweet potatoes

1 tsp salt

125ml/4 fl oz maple or golden syrup

1 tsp angostura bitters

1 tsp lemon juice

45g/1½ oz butter

Preparation time: 15 minutes
Cooking time: 30 minutes
Nutritional value:
Analysis per serving, approx:
• 1595kJ/380kcal
• 4g protein
• 7g fat
• 75g carbohydrate

Scrub the sweet potatoes under cold running water and boil, covered in water, for up to 30 minutes or until tender. • Test with a skewer or knife to see if they are cooked. Drain, cool slightly, peel, quarter and sprinkle with salt. • Heat the butter, syrup, angostura and lemon juice, stirring constantly. Add the sweet potatoes to this mixture, and reheat over a gentle heat, turning frequently, so that all surfaces are glazed. • Glazed Sweet Potatoes are a good accompaniment for roast lamb.

Our Tip: Use cooked sweet potatoes to make a spicy potato salad. Mix with thin slices of fresh celery and apple, skinned orange segments, chopped cashew nuts, a few raisins and a dressing made from mayonnaise and yogurt flavoured with curry powder.

Chicory Fritters

A festive side dish that can also be served as an entrée

8 medium-sized heads of chicory
2 lemons
2 l/3½ pints water
2 tsps salt
150g/5 ½oz flour
2 eggs
125ml/4 fl oz lager
1 tsp salt
1 tsp sugar
A bunch of parsley
1l/1¾ pints oil for deep-frying

Preparation time: 20 minutes
Cooking time: 10 minutes
Nutritional value:
Analysis per serving, approx:
• 1720kJ/410kcal
• 11g protein
• 24g fat
• 37g carbohydrate

Remove the outer leaves of chicory and trim the stems. Squeeze the lemons. • Add the salt and lemon juice to the water and bring to the boil. Add the chicory heads and boil for 10 minutes. • Drain well, and allow to cool. Wash the parsley and shake dry. • To make the batter, sift the flour into a bowl. Separate the eggs. Combine the egg yolks, beer, salt and sugar with the flour. • Heat the oil to 180°C/350°F in a deep-fryer or chip pan. • Beat the egg whites until stiff, and fold into the batter. • Coat the heads of chicory, a few at a time, with the batter, and fry in the hot oil until crisp and brown, turning from time to time. Lift out of the oil using a slotted spoon, and leave on absorbent kitchen paper to drain. Make sure the temperature of the oil reaches 180°C/350°F each time before putting in more fritters. • Keep the chicory fritters warm on a preheated serving plate. Put the parsley into the hot fat for 2-3 minutes, drain and use to garnish the fritters. • These go well with potato and herring salad or fried sliced ham.

Parsnip Croquettes

Parsnips are back in fashion!

Jerusalem Artichoke Fritters

A culinary revelation

600g/1lb 6oz parsnips

125ml/4 fl oz vegetable stock

75g/3oz cracked wheat

2 eggs

1 tbsp yeast extract

$^1/_2$ tsp salt

2 tbsps chopped parsley

5 tbsps safflower oil

Preparation time: 10 minutes
Cooking time: 1 hour
Nutritional value:
Analysis per serving, approx:
• 1365kJ/325kcal
• 8g protein
• 17g fat
• 35g carbohydrate

Peel or scrape the parsnips, wash thoroughly, dry and slice. Cook gently in the vegetable stock for up to 40 minutes or until tender. Add a little more vegetable stock or water if necessary to prevent them from sticking. • Purée the parsnips with the cooking liquid. Sprinkle the

cracked wheat over the purée. Add the eggs, yeast extract, salt and chopped parsley and work into a smooth dough. With damp hands, shape the dough into croquettes about the size of your palm. • Heat the oil. Fry the Parsnip Croquettes a few at a time until golden on both sides. Keep the cooked croquettes warm until all the dough has been used. • Lamb's lettuce salad goes well with these.

Our Tip: When cooked and drained, the parsnips may also be coated in batter as for Chicory Fritters, and fried until golden in plenty of oil. Parsnips cooked slowly in very little liquid and with 2 tbsp single cream added after cooking make a light vegetable side dish.

600g/1lb 6oz Jerusalem artichokes

1 tsp salt

1l/1$^3/_4$ pints water

$^1/_2$ red pepper

100g/4oz freshly crushed cracked wheat

$^1/_2$ tsp salt

1 tbsp sweet paprika

2 eggs

5 tbsps safflower oil

Preparation time: 30 minutes
Cooking time: 30 minutes
Nutritional value:
Analysis per serving, approx:
• 1490kJ/355kcal
• 10g protein
• 17g fat
• 40g carbohydrate

Wash, peel and slice the Jerusalem artichokes. Bring the salt and water to the boil. Boil the sliced Jerusalem artichokes for up to 20 minutes or until tender. •

Wash the pepper, remove the seeds and white pith, and chop finely. Combine the cracked wheat, salt, paprika and chopped pepper in a bowl. Separate the eggs. Mix the egg yolks and flour together, and add to the other ingredients in the bowl. Drain the Jerusalem artichokes well, chop finely and add to the bowl. Lastly, fold in the stiffly beaten egg whites. • Heat the oil in a frying-pan. Drop the batter into the pan a tablespoonful at a time, and flatten slightly. Fry the fritters until crisp and brown on both sides. Keep the cooked fritters warm until all the mixture has been used up. • Jerusalem Artichoke Fritters taste good with boiled chicken and Brussels sprouts

Different Ways of Serving Celeriac

Celeriac is a vegetable that deserves to be more popular

Celeriac in Sauce
Illustrated in background

800g/1³/₄lbs celeriac
A few celery leaves
2 tbsps vegetable margarine
250ml/8 fl oz hot water
1 tsp salt
¹/₂ tsp golden syrup
¹/₄ tsp white pepper
1 tbsp wholewheat flour
125ml/4 fl oz vegetable stock
¹/₂ tsp seasoned salt
1 egg yolk
4 tbsps sour cream or thick-set natural yogurt

Preparation time: 10 minutes
Cooking time: 30 minutes
Nutritional value:
Analysis per serving, approx:
• 630kJ/150kcal
• 5g protein
• 6g fat
• 17g carbohydrate

Scrub the celeriac under running water, peel, rinse again, cut into thick slices and then cut the slices into cubes. • Melt the margarine and sauté the celeriac until it begins to brown. Add the water, salt, syrup and pepper. Cover, and cook gently over a low heat until tender which should take about 25 minutes. • Sprinkle the flour over the celeriac, and then stir in the vegetable stock and herb-flavoured salt. Return the vegetables to the boil, and then simmer over a very low heat for another 5 minutes. • Wash and finely chop the celery leaves. Beat the egg yolk and sour cream together. • Remove the celeriac from the heat, cool slightly, and stir in the egg yolk and cream. Serve sprinkled with the chopped celery leaves.

Sliced Celeriac with Beef Marrow
Illustrated in foreground

1 large celeriac (700g/1lb 10oz)
A few celery leaves
Juice of 1 lemon
1 tsp sugar
1 tsp salt
2 large onions
50g/2oz butter
2 large beef marrowbones, available from butchers
2 pinches salt
¹/₂ tsp coarsely ground black pepper
2 tbsps chopped parsley

Preparation time: 10 minutes
Cooking time: 20 minutes
Nutritional value:
Analysis per serving, approx:
• 945kJ/225kcal
• 6g protein
• 12g fat
• 23g carbohydrate

Scrub the celeriac under running water, peel, rinse and slice. Cover with water, add the lemon juice, sugar and salt, bring to the boil and cook for 20 minutes, then drain. • Wash and finely chop the celery leaves, cover and reserve. • Peel and chop the onions, and brown in the butter. • Put the marrow bones into rapidly boiling water for 3 minutes, drain and extract the marrow from the bones. Halve each piece of marrow. Put the celeriac slices on a serving dish, arrange the fried onions over them, and put one piece of marrow on each portion. Season the marrow with salt and pepper, and sprinkle with the parsley and celery leaves. • Polenta, vegeburgers, or potatoes and green salad go well with this dish.

Glazed Spring Turnips

These baby turnips are especially succulent

800g/1³/₄lbs spring turnips
45g/1¹/₂oz butter
2 tbsps sugar
250ml/8 fl oz vegetable stock
¹/₄-¹/₂ tsp salt
Pinch white pepper
1 tsp cornflour
2 tbsps cream
2 tbsps chopped parsley

Preparation time: 15 minutes
Cooking time: 35 minutes
Nutritional value:
Analysis per serving, approx:
• 545kJ/130kcal
• 2g protein
• 7g fat
• 14g carbohydrate

Scrub the turnips thoroughly under running water, peel, rinse again and dry. Leave small turnips whole, cut larger ones into halves or quarters. • Melt the butter in a large saucepan. Dissolve the sugar in the butter, stirring constantly, until lightly browned. Sauté the turnips in this mixture for 5 minutes until they begin to colour. Heat the vegetable stock and pour it over the turnips. Cover and cook gently over a low heat for up to 30 minutes or until tender. • Season to taste with salt and pepper. Stir the cornflour into the cream, and use to thicken the sauce. • Turn the turnips into a preheated bowl, and sprinkle with the parsley. • This is a good accompaniment for baked potatoes and crisply fried slices of bacon.

Our Tip: From May to September there are various types of small white turnip in the shops, all of which are suitable for this dish.

Broccoli with Breadcrumbs Fried in Butter

This can easily be prepared in advance

1kg/2¹/₄lbs broccoli
125ml/4 fl oz vegetable stock
125ml/4 fl oz dry white wine
1 tsp salt
50g/2oz butter
100g/4oz fresh breadcrumbs

Preparation time: 15 minutes
Cooking time: 15 minutes
Nutritional value:
Analysis per serving, approx:
• 1155kJ/275kcal
• 12g protein
• 11g fat
• 29g carbohydrate

Wash the broccoli thoroughly under lukewarm running water, pick over and pat dry. Thinly peel the stalks, as for asparagus, from top to bottom, and separate from the florets. • Bring the vegetable stock to the boil with the wine and salt. Gently cook the stalks in this for 5 minutes, then add the florets, and cook for up to 10 minutes more or until done. • Heat the butter in a small saucepan. Fry the breadcrumbs in the butter, stirring frequently, until golden. Scatter over the broccoli before serving.

Our Tip: Depending on what is accompanying the broccoli, the fried breadcrumbs may be omitted and the broccoli topped with 125ml/4 fl oz single cream mixed with 100g/4oz freshly grated cheese. The broccoli should then be browned for 10 minutes in an oven preheated to 220°C/430°F/Gas Mark 6.

Brussel Sprouts with Chestnuts

A particularly elegant accompaniment, but also filling

800g/1³/₄lbs Brussels sprouts
1¹/₂ l/2¹/₂ pints water
1 tsp salt
400g/14oz chestnuts
1l/1³/₄ pints water
50g/2oz butter
2 tbsps honey
250ml/8 fl oz vegetable stock
Pinch each of salt and grated nutmeg

Preparation time: 20 minutes
Cooking time: 30 minutes
Nutritional value:
Analysis per serving, approx:
• 1825kJ/435kcal
• 13g protein
• 14g fat
• 64g carbohydrate

Remove the outer leaves of the Brussels sprouts, trim the stalks and wash. • Bring the salted water to the boil. Add the Brussels sprouts, cover and cook over a low heat for 20 minutes. • Bring the water for the chestnuts to the boil. Make an X-shaped incision at the pointed end of each chestnut, add to the boiling water, cover and boil briskly for 20 minutes. • Drain the Brussels sprouts in a colander. • Drain and peel the chestnuts and remove the inner skin. • Heat the butter and honey together, stirring constantly. Add the chestnuts to this mixture, turning to ensure they are well coated. Heat the vegetable stock, pour it over the chestnuts, cover and cook gently for 10 minutes. • Mix the Brussels sprouts with the chestnuts, and reheat thoroughly over an extremely low heat, then adjust the seasoning with salt and nutmeg. • A good accompaniment for lamb chops or roast venison.

Our Tip: If this is the only side dish being served with a roast, increase the quantity of chestnuts to 750g/1lb10oz.

Cabbage at its Best

Caraway and bacon are good flavouring for white or savoy cabbage

Caramelised Cabbage with Caraway Seeds

Illustrated in the background

1kg/2¹/₄lbs white cabbage
125ml/4 fl oz vegetable stock
100g/4oz clarified butter
2 tsps caster sugar
2 tsps caraway seeds
¹/₂ tsp salt

Preparation time: 15 minutes
Cooking time: 40 minutes
Nutritional value:
Analysis per serving, approx:
- 1260kJ/300kcal
- 4g protein
- 25g fat
- 14g carbohydrate

Remove the tough outer leaves of the cabbage. Cut in four, cut out the stalk, and separate the quarters into single leaves. Cut the leaves into broad strips. • Heat the vegetable stock. • Melt the clarified butter in a large shallow pan and dissolve the caster sugar in it. Put the strips of cabbage in the pan a few at a time, making sure each layer is properly coated before adding the next batch. Gradually add the vegetable stock, then the caraway seeds, cover and cook very slowly over a low heat for 40 minutes. • If necessary add a little water or vegetable stock during cooking to prevent the cabbage from sticking to the pan. Finally season the cabbage with salt. • This tastes good with roast pork or pork chops, meat loaf, rissoles or bratwurst sausages.

Our Tip: Instead of caraway, put in more sugar and season the cabbage with a little grated fresh ginger and soya sauce. If desired, 1-2 tbsps cornflour dissolved in a little wine vinegar may be used to thicken the sauce.

Savoy Cabbage with Bacon

Illustrated in the foreground

1kg/2¹/₄lbs Savoy cabbage
2 l/3¹/₂ pints water
1 tsp salt
250ml/8 fl oz vegetable stock
4 tbsps crème fraîche
2 tsps bottled green peppercorns
50g/2oz (4 thin rashers) streaky bacon
1 tbsp oil

Preparation time: 10 minutes
Cooking time: 25 minutes
Nutritional value:
Analysis per serving, approx:
- 905kJ/215kcal
- 8g protein
- 15g fat
- 11g carbohydrate

Discard the outer leaves of the cabbage, and cut into quarters. Rinse these in cold water. • Blanch the cabbage in the boiling salted water for 10 minutes. Heat the vegetable stock. • Preheat the oven to 220°C/430°F/Gas Mark 6. • Drain the cabbage quarters well and place in an ovenproof dish. Pour the vegetable stock over them. Mix the crème fraîche and the crushed peppercorns, and coat the cabbage with this mixture. • Cook, uncovered, for 15 minutes on the middle shelf of the oven. • Meanwhile, fry the sliced bacon in the oil until crisp. Drain on absorbent paper. Chop the bacon and sprinkle it over the cabbage before serving. • This dish goes well with parsley potatoes and fried breast of chicken.

Classic Ways with Cabbage and Sauerkraut

A fine accompaniment for roast beef, lamb and venison

Red Cabbage with Apple
Illustrated on the left

1kg/2¼lbs red cabbage
2 small cooking apples
25g/1oz clarified butter
125ml/4 fl oz vegetable stock
1 tsp salt
3 cloves
3 tbsps red wine vinegar
2 tbsps redcurrant jelly

Preparation time: 20 minutes
Cooking time: 1 hour
Nutritional value:
Analysis per serving, approx:
• 755kJ/180kcal
• 4g protein
• 6g fat
• 27g carbohydrate

Discard the coarse outer leaves of the red cabbage. Cut the cabbage in quarters, cut a wedge from the thick stalk and shred the quartered cabbage. Rinse the shredded cabbage in a colander under cold water and drain well. Quarter, peel and core the apples, and cut into thin slices. • Heat the vegetable stock. Melt the clarified butter and sauté the cabbage in it for 5 minutes. Add the hot vegetable stock, salt and cloves, cover and cook gently for 30 minutes over a low heat. If necessary, add a little water or vegetable stock to the cabbage as it cooks. • Add the apples and vinegar to the cabbage and continue cooking for a further 30 minutes. • When it is cooked, adjust the seasoning with the redcurrant jelly and a little more salt and red wine vinegar if necessary to give a delicate sweet-and-sour flavour. • This is a good accompaniment for roast venison or wildfowl, poultry, roast pork or pork chops.

Sauerkraut Cooked in Champagne
Illustrated on the right

1kg/2¼lbs sauerkraut
1 large onion
1 bay leaf
2 cloves
100g/4oz fatty bacon or smoked pork
2 tbsps oil
125ml/4 fl oz beef stock
125ml/4 fl oz dry white wine
Pinch each of salt and sugar
125ml/4 fl oz sparkling white wine

Preparation time: 10 minutes
Cooking time: 50 minutes
Nutritional value:
Analysis per serving, approx:
• 1430kJ/340kcal
• 7g protein
• 22g fat
• 17g carbohydrate

Use two forks to loosen and separate the sauerkraut. Peel the onion, and stick the bay leaf and cloves into it. Cut the bacon into 4 equal sized pieces. • Heat the oil and add the sauerkraut, turning so that it cooks on all sides. Heat the beef stock and pour over the sauerkraut. Add the onion with its spices, the pieces of bacon and the white wine, cover and braise over a medium heat for 50 minutes. • Remove the bacon and onion, and season the sauerkraut to taste with salt and sugar. Shortly before serving mix in the sparkling champagne or sparkling wine.

Our Tip: For a subtler flavour, omit the bacon and cook the sauerkraut with only the spiced onion. 10 minutes before serving, mix 200-300g/7-10oz fresh pineapple cut into small pieces into the sauerkraut and finally add the champagne.

Special Vegetable Dishes

Famous and lesser-known dishes from around the world, plus elegant pastry recipes for fortifying savoury flans, quiches and pizzas

Borscht

A hearty Russian soup containing beetroot and cabbage

1¹/₂l/2¹/₂ pints water
Salt and black pepper
500g/1lb 2oz stewing beef
100g/4oz bacon
500g/1lb 2oz white cabbage
500g/1lb 2oz raw beetroot
1 tbsp red wine vinegar
1 parsley root, or several stalks
¹/₄ celeriac
1 large onion
1 small leek
125ml/4fl oz sour cream
1 tbsp chopped parsley

Preparation time: 10 minutes
Cooking time: 1¹/₂ hours
Nutritional value:
Analysis per serving, approx:
- 1825kJ/435kcal
- 34g protein
- 22g fat
- 24g carbohydrate

Bring the water to the boil with the salt and pepper. Rinse the meat, add to the boiling water and bring back to the boil. Cook for 30 minutes, skimming off any scum that rises to the surface. • Remove the outer leaves from the cabbage, cut it into quarters, cut out the stalk and shred the leaves. Peel and wash the beetroot, reserving one root and cut the rest into strips. Grate the reserved beetroot and mix with the vinegar. Peel or scrape the parsley root and the celeriac, wash and cut into small dice. Peel and chop the onion. Trim and wash the leek, and slice the white part only into thin slices. • After 40 minutes boiling, add all the prepared vegetables except the grated beetroot to the meat. Cover the pan and continue cooking over a low heat for up to another 50 minutes or until tender. • Remove the meat and cut into cubes. Return the meat, together with the reserved grated beetroot, to the soup and reheat. • Serve a dollop of sour cream on each helping of soup, and sprinkle with parsley.

Hearty Provençal Soup

This is more of a stew than a soup and is a main course in itself

2 leeks
2 onions
400g/14oz potatoes
4 large tomatoes
2 cloves garlic
1 bulb fennel
3 tbsps olive oil
500-750ml/16-24fl oz hot vegetable stock
¹/₂ tsp salt
Pinch of cayenne
1 tbsp chopped parsley

Preparation time: 30 minutes
Cooking time: 30 minutes
Nutritional value:
Analysis per serving, approx:
- 1155kJ/275kcal
- 9g protein
- 9g fat
- 39g carbohydrate

Trim the root and the dark green leaves from the leeks, halve them lengthways, wash and slice. Peel and chop the onions. Remove the hard stalk ends from the tomatoes, pour boiling water over them, skin and dice. Peel, wash and slice the potatoes. Peel and crush the garlic. Discard the tough outer leaves of the fennel, and shred. • Heat the olive oil in a large saucepan, first sauté the diced onion and sliced leek then add the sliced potato, diced tomato, crushed garlic and shredded fennel and sauté for a few more minutes. Pour over the vegetable stock and cook for up to 30 minutes until tender. • Then push the soup through a sieve or blend in a liquidizer, and season to taste with the salt and cayenne. • Serve the soup sprinkled with the parsley.

Our Tip: In Provence, the soup is served in soup plates or cups with slices of fried French bread which are floated on the soup just before serving. The parsley is then sprinkled over the bread.

Andalusian Gazpacho

A refreshing chilled vegetable soup

500g/1lb 2oz tomatoes
2 onions
2 large cloves garlic
1 cucumber (about 500g/1lb 2oz)
1 large green pepper
500ml/16 fl oz water
2 tbsps wine vinegar
2 tbsps olive oil
50g/2oz dry white breadcrumbs
1 tbsp tomato purée
1 tsp salt
Good pinch each of black pepper and sugar
150g/5¹/₂oz stale white bread
25g/1oz butter
1 large onion

Preparation time: 15 minutes
Standing time: 2 hours
Nutritional value:
Analysis per serving, approx:
• 1535kJ/365kcal
• 11g protein
• 11g fat
• 56g carbohydrate

Remove the hard stalk ends from the tomatoes. Pour boiling water over them, peel and cut into eight sections. Peel and roughly chop the onions and garlic. Wash and dry the cucumber and pepper. Cut half of the cucumber into fairly large cubes. Halve the pepper, discard the pith and seeds, and dice. Purée the prepared vegetables in a liquidiser or food processor and add the water, vinegar, oil, breadcrumbs and tomato purée into this mixture with the motor running. • Season liberally with salt, pepper and sugar. • Place the Gazpacho in the refrigerator and leave for 2 hours. • Cut the white bread into small cubes and fry these until golden in the melted butter, then allow to cool. Peel and finely chop the onion. Dice the remaining half of the cucumber. • Serve the croûtons, chopped onion and diced cucumber separately to accompany the Gazpacho.

Tarator

Cold cucumber soup for a hot summer's day

3 cloves garlic
1 tsp salt
4 tbsps olive oil
1kg/2¹/₄lbs cucumber
600ml/1pt thick-set natural yogurt
125ml/4 fl oz sour cream
¹/₄ tsp each salt and white pepper
4 tsps finely chopped dill
2 tbsps ground hazelnuts

Preparation time: 10 minutes
Standing time: 2 hours
Nutritional value:
Analysis per serving, approx:
• 1195kJ/285kcal
• 8g protein
• 21g fat
• 16g carbohydrate

Peel and chop the garlic, and crush with the salt. Stir the olive oil into the crushed garlic a drop at a time. Peel the cucumber, grate it, and combine with the yogurt, sour cream and crushed garlic. Season to taste with salt and pepper, cover and leave to stand for at least 2 hours in a cool place. • Before serving, put 2 ice cubes in each bowl, and sprinkle the soup with the chopped dill and ground hazelnuts.

Our Tip: For an even lower calorie count, use low-fat yogurt instead of whole-milk yogurt. The soup becomes American rather than Bulgarian if instead of cucumber you use 1kg/2¹/₄lbs beefsteak tomatoes simmered gently in 4 tbsps oil without any garlic, then sieved, brought back to the boil with 2 tsps cornflour dissolved in cold water, chilled, then mixed with yogurt and sour cream.

Classic Vegetable Stews

Prawns and beef complement these vegetables well

Finnish Vegetable Stew
Illustrated in the background

1¼l/2½ pints water • Salt
1 small cauliflower
2 large carrots
400g/14oz potatoes
200g/7oz green beans
5 radishes
200g/7oz shelled peas
200g/7oz spinach
2 tbsps flour • 2 tbsps soft butter
¼ tsp each sugar and white pepper
400g/14oz cooked prawns or crayfish tails
5 tbsps single cream
2 tbsps chopped dill

Preparation time: 30 minutes
Cooking time: 20 minutes
Nutritional value:
Analysis per serving, approx:
• 1595kJ/380kcal • 29g protein
• 11g fat • 41g carbohydrate

Bring some salted water to the boil. • Remove the outer green leaves from the cauliflower. Break into florets, wash thoroughly in cold water and drain. Scrape and dice the carrots. Peel, wash and dice the potatoes. Wash the green beans, top and tail them, and cut into pieces. Wash the radishes, top and tail them and cut them into quarters. • Put all these vegetables and the peas into the boiling water, cover, and cook for up to 15 minutes or until tender. • Wash the spinach and pick it over, chop roughly, add to the stew and cook for 5 minutes. Transfer the vegetables to a colander, reserving the cooking water. • Knead the flour into the butter. Add to the vegetable water and beat with an egg whisk until it has dissolved, then cook for 5 minutes. Season the sauce to taste with the salt, sugar and pepper. Heat the prawns or crayfish in the sauce. Return the vegetables to it, and reheat thoroughly. • Stir the cream into the stew, and serve sprinkled with the dill.

Garbure
A French casserole from Béarn
Illustrated in the foreground

1½l/2½ pints water
1 tsp salt
500g/1lb 2oz brisket of beef
½ onion
1 bay leaf
1 large carrot
4 white turnips
400g/14oz potatoes
200g/7oz white cabbage
250g/8oz green beans
1 bunch parsley
A sprig of lovage
2 stalks chervil
¼ tsp each salt and white pepper

Preparation time: 10 minutes
Cooking time: 70 minutes

Nutritional value:
Analysis per serving, approx:
• 1220kJ/290kcal
• 28g protein
• 8g fat
• 26g carbohydrate

Add the salt to the water and bring to the boil. Place the brisket of beef in the water. Add the onion and bay leaf, and cook in an uncovered saucepan for 30 minutes, continually skimming off any scum that forms. • Dice the carrot, turnips and peeled potatoes, shred the cabbage, and cut the beans into pieces. Chop 1 tbsp of the parsley and reserve it. • After the beef has been cooking for 30 minutes, add all the vegetables except the reserved parsley, the sprig of lovage and the chervil to the pot and continue to cook for another 40 minutes. • Lift out the meat, cut into cubes, and return to the saucepan. Adjust the seasoning, and sprinkle with the reserved parsley.

Sauerkraut with a Difference

Hearty, substantial – and irresistible

Alsatian Choucroûte
Illustrated on the left

Ingredients for 8 portions:

2kg/4¹/₂lbs sauerkraut
1 onion • 1 bay leaf
2 cloves • 1 clove garlic
5 juniper berries
500ml/16 fl oz dry white wine, from Alsace
4 tbsps goose fat or bacon fat
¹/₂ tsp salt
8 small potatoes
200g/7oz streaky bacon
600g/1lb 6oz pickled loin of pork
8 knackwurst sausages

Preparation time: 10 minutes
Cooking time: 2 hours
Nutritional value:
Analysis per serving, approx:
- 2750kJ/655kcal
- 30g protein
- 55g fat
- 19g carbohydrate

Rinse the sauerkraut in lukewarm water, squeeze out excess moisture and put into a saucepan large enough to hold it comfortably. • Peel the onion and stick the bay leaf and cloves into it. Peel the garlic. Add these and the juniper berries and white wine to the sauerkraut. Add 250-500ml/8-16 fl oz of water. Mix the goose or bacon fat and salt into the sauerkraut, cover and cook together for 2 hours, turning the vegetables over from time to time. • Peel and wash the potatoes; after 1¹/₂ hours add these to the sauerkraut and continue cooking. Put the bacon, loin of pork and sausages into boiling water, and heat through for 30 minutes, keeping the water on the boil. • Remove the onion and the clove of garlic from the saucepan. Transfer the sauerkraut to a serving plate, with the potatoes arranged round the edge. Slice the meat and sausages and arrange over the choucroûte.

Hungarian Cabbage Rolls
Illustrated on the right

100g/4oz long-grain rice
1 l/1³/₄ pints water • Salt
1 small white cabbage
1 small onion
400g/14oz lean minced pork
1 egg • ¹/₄ tsp paprika
2 tbsps lard
500g/1lb 2oz sauerkraut
2 tbsps tomato purée
125ml/4 fl oz water
125ml/4 fl oz sour cream

Preparation time: 20 minutes
Cooking time: 40 minutes
Nutritional value:
Analysis per serving, approx:
- 2520kJ/600kcal • 27g protein
- 39g fat • 36g carbohydrate

Wash the rice, and boil in salted water until done. • Drain well. Remove 12 large leaves from the white cabbage (reserve the rest for another dish), and blanch them in boiling salted water for 5 minutes. Then drain, and pare the large ribs to produce a flat surface. • Preheat the oven to 200°C/400°F/Gas Mark 6. • Peel and chop the onions. Mix together the minced pork, chopped onion, egg, some salt, paprika and rice. • Place 3 cabbage leaves on top of one another, put a quarter of the stuffing on top, and roll up, securing with kitchen string, or a wooden cocktail stick; repeat with the remaining leaves, making a total of 4 rolls. • Melt the butter in a flameproof dish, and fry the stuffed cabbage leaves gently; then remove them and replace with the sauerkraut. • Combine the tomato purée and water and stir into the sauerkraut. Lay the cabbage rolls on top, and bake for 40 minutes. • Pour the sour cream over the dish.

Ratatouille

The classic vegetable casserole from Provence

1 medium-sized aubergine	
2 tsps salt	
500g/1lb 2oz courgettes	
2 onions	
2 red and 1 yellow peppers (about 400g/14oz)	
4 large beefsteak tomatoes	
10 tbsps olive oil	
3 cloves garlic	
1/2 tsp ground coriander	
1 tsp chopped basil	
1/4 tsp each salt and black pepper	
125-250ml/4-8 fl oz vegetable stock	
1 tbsp chopped parsley	

Preparation time: 50 minutes
Cooking time: 45 minutes
Nutritional value:
Analysis per serving, approx:
- 1660kJ/395kcal
- 8g protein
- 27g fat
- 30g carbohydrate

Cut the aubergine into 1cm/1/2-inch slices. Sprinkle salt over the slices, arrange on a plate, weighed down with another plate and leave for 30 minutes. Discard the bitter juice, rinse and dry the aubergines. • Slice the courgettes. Peel and chop the onions. Cut the peppers in strips. Pour boiling water over the tomatoes, skin and dice them. • Heat 2 tbsps of the oil in a frying-pan, and sauté each vegetable except the tomatoes without browning, adding more oil as required. Peel and finely chop the garlic. Combine the fried vegetables with the garlic, coriander, basil, salt and pepper. Place in a saucepan and add enough vegetable stock to give a depth of about 2cm/3/4 inch. Cover the pan and braise the vegetables over a low heat for 30 minutes. • Then add the tomatoes and parsley and cook for another 15 minutes or until done. • Serve with French bread. Lamb chops make a good accompaniment.

Hungarian Vegetable Stew

This stew, the finest way of serving tomatoes and peppers, is called Lecsó in Hungarian

500g/1lb 2oz tomatoes	
500g/1lb 2oz green and yellow peppers	
2 large onions	
4 rashers green or smoked streaky bacon	
1 tbsp sweet paprika	
1/2 tsp salt	
1/4 tsp black pepper	

Preparation time: 20 minutes
Cooking time: 30 minutes
Nutritional value:
Analysis per serving, approx:
- 1070kJ/225kcal
- 7g protein
- 17g fat
- 18g carbohydrate

Remove the hard stalk ends from the tomatoes, pour boiling water over them, skin and cut into chunks. Halve the peppers, remove the pith and seeds, wash, dry and cut into smaller pieces. Peel and slice the onions, then quarter the slices.

• Dice the bacon, and fry in a dry frying-pan until the fat runs. Sauté the onion in the bacon fat until golden. Add the peppers, and sauté together for 5 minutes. • Combine the tomato, paprika, salt and pepper with the other vegetables, cover and cook over a low heat for up to 30 minutes or until done. • Serve with boiled rice and Hungarian or Polish boiling sausage.

Our Tip: There is no hard and fast rule regarding the types of vegetables used for Lecsó. It can be made with red peppers and a piece of cucumber, or a few courgettes may be added.

Chinese Stir-fry Vegetables

Vegetables cooked quickly in a wok

8 dried Chinese mushrooms (cloud ears)
500ml/16 fl oz hot water
4 spring onions
300g/10oz celery
300g/10oz carrots
300g/10oz red peppers
150g/5½oz each canned bamboo shoots and bean sprouts
1 small clove garlic
1 small piece fresh root ginger (about 20g/¾oz)
5 tbsps sesame oil
4 tbsps soy sauce
½ tsp salt
¼ tsp each sugar and black pepper

Preparation time: 40 minutes
Cooking time: 15 minutes
Nutritional value:
Analysis per serving, approx:
- 1010kJ/2405kcal
- 6g protein
- 14g fat
- 22g carbohydrate

Soak the dried mushrooms in the hot water for 30 minutes allowing them to swell. • Prepare the spring onions, celery and carrots, wash and cut into julienne strips. Halve the peppers, remove the pith and seeds, wash and cut into thin strips. Slice the bamboo and bean sprouts thinly; cut the bamboo shoots into small slices. Peel, chop and crush the garlic. Peel and grate the ginger. • Heat the oil in a wok or large frying-pan. Sauté the garlic, ginger and onion. • Reserve 125ml/4 fl oz of the water in which the mushrooms have been soaked. Squeeze excess moisture out of the mushrooms, and quarter them. • Add the celery, carrots and mushrooms to the vegetables in the wok, and cook for 4 minutes. • Pour the reserved soaking water over the vegetables. Add the pepper, and cook for a further 6 minutes or until the vegetables are tender. • Season well with the soy sauce, salt, sugar and pepper. Mix in the bamboo sprouts and bean shoots. • Heat through for another 3 minutes. • Chinese noodles and medallions of pork make a good accompaniment.

Potatoes Combined with Other Vegetables

A colourful mixture that harmonises well

Neapolitan Vegetable Casserole
Illustrated in background

500g/1lb 2oz aubergines	
2 tsps salt	
2 yellow peppers	
4 beefsteak tomatoes	
600g/1lb 6oz potatoes	
2 large onions	
2 cloves garlic	
125ml/4 fl oz olive oil	
4 leaves fresh basil	
1 tsp salt	
¼ tsp black pepper	
2 tbsps chopped chives	

Preparation time: 40 minutes
Cooking time: 40-50 minutes
Nutritional value:
Analysis per serving, approx:
- 2245kJ/535kcal
- 10g protein
- 33g fat
- 49g carbohydrate

Thinly peel the aubergines, halve lengthways, and cut the halves into 2cm/³/₄-inch strips. Sprinkle salt over the sliced aubergine, and leave covered for 30 minutes. • Preheat the oven to 200°C/400°F/Gas Mark 6. • Prepare the peppers and cut into strips. Pour boiling water over the tomatoes, skin and cut into chunks, removing the hard stalk ends. Peel the potatoes and cut into sticks about 2cm/³/₄inch in diameter. Peel the onions, and cut them also into strips. Peel and finely chop the garlic. • Discard the liquid that has been drawn from the aubergines. • Heat the oil in a flameproof dish with a lid. Sauté the onion and garlic until transparent, and add the prepared vegetables. Shred the basil leaves, and stir them into the vegetables with the pepper and salt. • Cover the casserole and cook on the lowest shelf of the oven for about 40-50 minutes until done. • Scatter the chives on top before serving. • Smoked bratwurst or other smoked continental sausages taste good with this casserole.

Onions au Gratin, Swiss Style
Illustrated in foreground

600g/1lb 6oz each potatoes and onions	
1 tsp salt	
½ tsp coarsely ground black pepper	
250ml/8 fl oz vegetable stock	
125ml/4 fl oz cream	
150g/6oz Gruyère cheese, freshly grated	
45g/1½ oz butter	
1 tbsp chopped parsley	

Preparation time: 45 minutes
Cooking time: 55 minutes
Nutritional value:
Analysis per serving, approx:
- 1955kJ/465kcal
- 17g protein
- 28g fat
- 36g carbohydrate

Preheat the oven to 220°C/430°F/Gas Mark 7. Peel the potatoes and onions and slice thinly. • Arrange the potato and onion slices in alternating layers in an ovenproof dish, seasoning each layer with salt and pepper. Pour the vegetable stock over them. • Bake in the oven for up to 40 minutes or until tender. • Mix the cream and grated cheese and pour this mixture over the vegetables. Put dabs of butter on top, and continue cooking for up to another 15 minutes until the topping is golden. • Serve sprinkled with the parsley. • A fresh mixed salad makes a good accompaniment.

Typical Dishes from Across the Channel

These are the ways in which European cousins cook their favourite vegetables

Chicory, Brussels Style

Illustrated in background

4 heads of chicory of equal size
1½ l/2½ pints water
1½ tsps salt • 1 tbsp lemon juice
500g/1lb 2oz, breast of chicken, skinned and boned
45g/1½oz butter
1 tbsp flour
250ml/8 fl oz chicken stock
125ml/4 fl oz single cream
Pinch of grated nutmeg
¼ tsp white pepper
4 slices lean cooked ham
2 egg yolks
4 tbsps grated Gouda cheese

Preparation time: 30 minutes
Cooking time: 25 minutes
Nutritional value:
Analysis per serving, approx:
• 2060kJ/490kcal • 43g protein
• 32g fat • 8g carbohydrate

Preheat the oven to 200°C/400°F/Gas Mark 6. Trim the root end of the chicory. Bring the water to the boil with 1 tsp of the salt and the lemon juice. Simmer the heads of chicory for 15 minutes. • Cut the chicken breasts into small cubes, and sauté in 25g/1oz of the butter for 6 minutes. • In another saucepan, melt the remaining butter and add the flour. Cook, stirring, for 2 minutes then add the chicken stock to make a white sauce, stirring constantly. Bring to the boil, then reduce the heat and simmer for 10 minutes. • Add the cream, nutmeg, the rest of the salt, pepper and diced chicken to the sauce. • Halve the chicory, and fill one half of each head with some fricasséed chicken. Place the other half over it, and wrap a slice of ham round each stuffed head of chicory. Place in an ovenproof dish. Incorporate the egg yolks and cheese into the remaining fricassée, and pour this over the chicory. • Cook in the oven for 10 minutes or until browned.

Italian Courgette Bake

Illustrated in foreground

4 medium-sized courgettes (800g/1¾lbs)
1½ l/2½ pints water
2½ tsps salt
2 yellow peppers
4 tomatoes • 2 cloves garlic
2 sprigs fresh basil
8 anchovy fillets, soaked in water for 2 hours and drained
3 tbsps olive oil
150g/5½oz Fontina cheese, thinly sliced

Preparation time: 30 minutes
Cooking time: 30-35 minutes
Nutritional value:
Analysis per serving, approx:
• 1470kJ/350kcal • 17g protein
• 23g fat • 19g carbohydrate

Preheat the oven to 200°C/400°F/Gas Mark 6. Wash the courgettes, then drain. Trim the stalk ends and halve lengthways. Bring the salted water to the boil. Blanch the halved courgettes for 5 minutes, drain, arrange in an ovenproof dish and sprinkle with salt. • Roast the peppers on the hot electric hob on all sides. Then peel off the skin, halve, remove the pith and seeds, and cut into strips. Pour boiling water over the tomatoes, skin and cut into pieces. Peel and finely chop the garlic. Wash the basil, pat dry and shred the leaves. Cut the anchovy fillets in half lengthways. • Heat 2 tbsps oil. Sauté the garlic, basil and vegetables, season with salt and simmer in a covered pan for about 10 minutes. Pile this mixture on top of the courgettes. Top first with the strips of anchovy then the cheese, drizzling the remaining oil over the top. • Bake in the oven for 20-25 minutes or until cooked.

Chilli con Carne

A fiery beef and bean stew

Ingredients for 6 portions:

350g/11oz dried red kidney beans
2 onions
2 cloves garlic
50g/2oz lard
500g/1lb 2oz coarsely ground beef
2 tsps salt
¹/₂ tsp black pepper
¹/₂-1 tsp chilli powder
1 small red dried chilli
1 tbsp sweet paprika
500ml/16 fl oz tomato juice

Standing time: 12 hours
Preparation time: 20 minutes
Cooking time: 1¹/₂ hours
Nutritional value:
Analysis per serving, approx:
• 1745kJ/415kcal
• 31g protein
• 15g fat
• 39g carbohydrate

Wash the beans and pick them over, then leave to soak for 12 hours covered in fresh water. Drain. • Peel and finely chop the onion and garlic. Dice the lard and heat it in a deep pan. Fry the chopped onion and garlic in the lard until golden. Add the minced meat and fry until it changes colour. Then add the beans, the salt, pepper, chilli powder, crushed chilli, paprika and tomato juice. Cook, uncovered, over a low heat for 1¹/₂ hours. Stir frequently while the chilli is cooking, adding more tomato juice if necessary to prevent sticking.

Our Tip: If you are in a hurry you can use 500g/1lb 2oz canned red beans; you can then reduce the cooking time to just 20 minutes before you have the Chilli con Carne on the table. – If you wish, you can add 3-4 skinned diced tomatoes to the pan 10 minutes before the dish is ready.

Moussaka

One of the most versatile of vegetable dishes

2 onions, chopped
5 beefsteak tomatoes
2 cloves garlic, finely chopped
500g/1lb 2oz aubergine
75g/3oz butter
200g/7oz each minced beef and pork
250ml/8 fl oz dry white wine
2 tbsps chopped parsley
1/2 tsp each salt and white pepper
1/2 tsp each dried thyme and rosemary
2 tbsps olive oil
4 tbsps flour
750ml/1 1/4 pints warm milk
1/2 tsp each salt and white pepper
50g/2oz freshly grated Gruyère cheese

Preparation time: 30 minutes
Cooking time: 1 hour 10 mins
Nutritional value:
Analysis per serving, approx:
• 2310kJ/550kcal • 25g protein
• 33g fat • 31g carbohydrate

Preheat the oven to 200°C/ 400°F/Gas Mark 6. Pour boiling water over 4 of the tomatoes, skin and dice. Thinly slice the remaining tomato. Wash the aubergines and slice lengthways. • Sauté the onion in 25g/1oz of the butter until it is transparent. Add the mince and let it brown slightly. Then add the white wine, the diced tomatoes, parsley, salt, pepper, thyme, rosemary and garlic. Cover the pan and cook for 40 minutes. • Fry the sliced aubergine in the oil until it begins to brown. • Melt the rest of the butter and add the flour. Cook stirring constantly for 2 minutes then add the milk to make a white sauce. Season to taste and simmer gently for 10 minutes. • Arrange alternating layers of sliced aubergine, mince and white sauce in an ovenproof dish, finishing with a layer of white sauce. Sprinkle the cheese on top. • Bake for about 30 minutes.

Turkish Aubergine Casserole

A particularly delicious way of preparing aubergines

600g/1lb 6oz small aubergines
1 1/2 tbsps salt
3 onions
1 clove garlic
2 beefsteak tomatoes
500g/1lb 2oz boned shoulder of veal
15g/1/2oz butter
3 tbsps sesame oil
1/2 tsp coarsely ground black pepper
500ml/16 fl oz beef stock

Preparation time: 45 minutes
Cooking time: 50 minutes
Nutritional value:
Analysis per serving, approx:
• 1345kJ/320kcal
• 30g protein
• 13g fat
• 20g carbohydrate

Wash and slice the aubergines, sprinkle with 1 tsp of the salt and leave to stand for 30 minutes. • Peel and chop the onions and crush the garlic. Pour boiling water over the tomatoes, skin and chop finely. Cut the meat into 2cm/1-inch cubes. • Rinse the sliced aubergine in cold water and pat dry. • Heat the butter and oil in a large frying-pan with a lid. Fry the sliced aubergine until it is light brown, and drain on absorbent kitchen paper. Sauté the chopped onion in the fat until transparent, add the meat and fry until crisp. Add the garlic and tomatoes, and season with the remainder of the salt and the pepper. Heat the beef stock and pour it over the meat. Cover and simmer for 30 minutes. • Return the aubergines to the frying-pan and cook for up to another 20 minutes or until done. • Rice makes a good accompaniment to this dish.

Onion Flan

Almost every wine-growing region has its own version of this delicious pie

Ingredients for 15-slice flan:

FOR THE BASE:

400g/14oz flour
40g/1½oz fresh yeast or 20g/½oz dried yeast
Pinch of sugar
185ml/5 fl oz lukewarm milk
50g/2oz butter
½ tsp salt

FOR THE FILLING:

1 ½kg/3lbs 6oz onions
1 clove garlic
1 tsp salt
200g/7oz streaky bacon
4 tbsps oil
125ml/4 fl oz dry white wine
¼ tsp white pepper
½ tsp crushed caraway seeds
1 tsp dried rosemary
3 eggs
3 tbsps sour cream
2 tbsps breadcrumbs
150g/5½oz Cheddar cheese, freshly grated
Butter or oil for the baking sheet

Preparation time including standing time: 1½ hours
Cooking time: 40 minutes
Nutritional value:

Analysis per slice, approx:

- 1450kJ/345kcal
- 11g protein
- 20g fat
- 30g carbohydrate

Sift the flour into a bowl, make a well in the middle, and crumble the yeast into it. Sprinkle the sugar over the yeast, and pour in the lukewarm milk. Stir the yeast into some of the flour and milk. Sprinkle a little flour over the yeast mixture, cover with an upturned bowl and leave to stand for 15 minutes or until the flour covering the yeast is beginning to crack. • Cut the butter into small pieces and cut these into the edges of the flour. Sprinkle with the salt and then work all the ingredients in the bowl, including the yeast, into a smooth dough. Continue to knead the dough until it begins to produce bubbles and comes away cleanly from the sides of the bowl, then leave to stand in a warm place for at least 30 minutes or until the dough had doubled in bulk. • Meanwhile, peel the onions and cut into thin rings. Peel the garlic, chop up small, and crush with the salt. Dice the bacon. • Heat the oil in a large saucepan. Add the sliced onion and sauté until transparent. Pour the wine over the onions. Add the pepper, caraway seeds, crushed rosemary and garlic. Simmer, covered, over a low heat for 20 minutes. • Fry the bacon in a dry frying-pan until the fat runs. Grease the baking sheet. • Roll out the risen dough to fit the baking sheet, place on the sheet and leave for another 20 minutes to rise again. Preheat the oven to 200°C/400°F/Gas Mark 6. • Beat the eggs with the sour cream and breadcrumbs, and stir into the onions. Spread the onion mixture evenly over the dough, scatter the fried, diced bacon over it, and top with the grated cheese. • Bake the flan for 40 minutes. • Cut into 15 pieces while it is still hot. Serve warm.

Our Tip: For an Alsace-style Onion Flan, make a short-crust pastry from 400g/14oz plain flour, 150-200g/5½-7oz butter, 1 tsp salt, 1 egg and sufficient water to produce a pliable dough. In Alsace, the onion mixture is seasoned with salt, pepper and grated nutmeg, and only about 100g/4oz streaky bacon is used, but 100ml/3 fl oz crème fraîche is added along with the eggs.

Italian Celery Flan

Serve with new wine

Ingredients for a 26cm/10-inch flan (12 slices):

FOR THE DOUGH:

200g/7oz plain flour
60g/2oz cooking fat
³/₄ tsp salt
125ml/4 fl oz water (scant measure)

FOR THE FILLING:

700g/1¹/₂lbs celery
500ml/16 fl oz water
2 medium-sized onions
4 eggs
3 tbsps single cream
100g/4oz Parmesan cheese, freshly grated
¹/₄ tsp white pepper
Pinch each of grated nutmeg and salt
Fat for greasing the tin

Preparation time: 30 minutes
Cooking time: 40 minutes
Nutritional value:
Analysis per slice, approx:
• 800kJ/190kcal
• 8g protein
• 10g fat
• 17g carbohydrate

Grease a 26cm/10-inch springform tin. • Work the flour, cooking fat, salt and water into a smooth dough. Roll out the pastry and line the base and sides of the tin. Leave in the refrigerator to rest for at least 30 minutes. • Preheat the oven to 220°C/430°F/Gas Mark 7. • Trim the celery, wash it, halve the stalks lengthways and cut into small pieces. Bring the salted water to the boil, and cook the celery for 8 minutes. Peel and finely chop the onions. • Drain the celery. Beat the eggs with the cream. Stir in the pieces of celery, the chopped onion and the Parmesan cheese. Season liberally with pepper, nutmeg and salt. Pour the mixture into the pastry base. • Bake on the middle shelf of the oven for 40 minutes. • Serve piping hot.

Greek Spinach Pie

A tasty filling in a paper-thin crust

Ingredients for 10 slices:

300g/10oz filo dough sheets
1kg/2¹/₄lbs spinach
1l/1³/₄ pints water • 1 tsp salt
1 bunch spring onions or 5 shallots • 1 clove garlic
50g/2oz butter
¹/₄ tsp each salt and white pepper
Pinch of grated nutmeg
200g/7oz Feta cheese • 4 eggs
5 tbsps fresh breadcrumbs
1 egg yolk • Melted butter

Preparation time: 1 hour
Cooking time: 50 minutes
Nutritional value:
Analysis per slice, approx:
• 1175kJ/280kcal • 14g protein
• 16g fat • 19g carbohydrate

Defrost the phyllo dough. • Pick over the spinach, then wash it. Bring the salted water to the boil. Blanch the spinach for 4 minutes, drain and chop coarsely. • Peel and finely chop the spring onions or shallots and the garlic, and sauté in the melted butter until transparent. Add the spinach. Season the vegetables. • Dice the cheese. Beat the eggs, and mix into the spinach with the breadcrumbs and cheese . • Preheat the oven to 200°C/400°F/Gas Mark 6. Rinse a baking sheet in cold water. • Defrost the dough, if frozen. Cut out 6 rectangles measuring 25x30cm/10x12 inches. Brush 3 sheets of dough with melted butter and arrange over half of the baking sheet so that they overlap the edge. Arrange the spinach on top and fold the overhanging edges in to the centre to partially cover the filling. Brush the remaining sheets of dough with melted butter and lay them on top; pierce several holes in the pastry lid with the tines of a fork. Brush the top of the pie with more melted butter and the beaten egg yolk, and bake for 50 minutes or until golden.

Leek Flan

A substantial main course cooked in the oven

Tomato and Crème Fraîche Flan

A good starter

Ingredients for a 26cm/10-inch flan (10 slices):

FOR THE DOUGH:

250g/8oz plain flour, sifted

Pinch of salt

1 egg

100g/4oz butter, cut into small pieces

FOR THE FILLING:

600g/1lb 6oz leeks

200g/7oz streaky bacon

1 tbsp oil

Pinch of curry powder

200g/7oz mortadella

2 eggs

250ml/8 fl oz sour cream

Salt and black pepper

Preparation time: 15 minutes
Standing time: 1 hour
Cooking time: 45 minutes
Nutritional value:
Analysis per slice, approx:
• 1720kJ/410kcal • 12g protein
• 31g fat • 21g carbohydrate

To make the dough, knead the sifted flour, salt, egg and butter together. Cover and leave in the refrigerator to rest for 1 hour. • Slit the leeks in half lengthways, wash thoroughly, cut off the dark green ends and the roots, and slice the remaining white part. • Dice the bacon, and fry in the oil until golden. Add the leeks, season with salt, pepper and curry powder, cover, and braise over a low heat for 10 minutes. • Preheat the oven to 200°C/400°F/Gas Mark 6. • Roll out the dough, and use it to line the base and sides of a 26cm/10-inch springform tin. Pierce the pastry in several places with a fork. Dice the mortadella and distribute the pieces over the dough, then add the leek mixture. Beat the eggs, sour cream, salt and pepper together, and pour the mixture over the leeks. • Bake the flan on the middle shelf of the oven for 45 minutes.

Ingredients for a 26cm/10-inch flan (8 slices):

200g/7oz frozen puff dough

600g/1lb 6oz tomatoes

3 eggs

1/4 tsp each salt and white pepper

1/2 tsp freshly chopped basil

5 tbsps crème fraîche

15g/1/2oz butter, melted

5 tbsps freshly grated Cheddar cheese

Preparation time including thawing time: 40 minutes
Cooking time: 33 minutes
Nutritional value:
Analysis per slice, approx:
• 860kJ/205kcal
• 8g protein
• 14g fat
• 12g carbohydrate

Unwrap the frozen dough and leave to defrost; then roll out into a circle on a floured work surface. • Rinse a 26cm/10-inch springform tin in cold water. Lay the dough in the tin, raising the edge slightly to make a rim. Leave to rest in the refrigerator for 30 minutes. Preheat the oven to 200°C/400°F/Gas Mark 6. • Remove the hard stalk ends from the tomatoes, pour boiling water over them, skin and cut into small pieces. Arrange the tomatoes on the pastry base. Beat the eggs with the salt, pepper and basil. Gradually stir in the crème fraîche and the melted butter. Pour this mixture over the tomatoes, and sprinkle the grated cheese over the filling. • Cook on the middle shelf of the oven for 8 minutes. Lower the heat to 180°C/350°F/Gas Mark 4, and cook for up to another 25 minutes until golden brown. • If the topping becomes too brown before the flan is cooked, cover it with greaseproof paper or aluminium foil. • Serve piping hot.

Swiss Chard Flan with a Cheese Topping

A perfect meal – and not only for vegetarians

Quantities for a 26cm/10-inch flan (8 slices):

1kg/2 ¼lbs Swiss chard

3l/5¼ pints water

1 tsp salt

100g/4oz softened butter

4 egg yolks

250g/8oz low-fat curd cheese

125ml/4 fl oz single cream

150g/5 ½oz plain flour

3 tbsps semolina

½ tsp salt

¼ tsp grated nutmeg

50g/2oz fresh breadcrumbs

100g/4oz Cheddar cheese, freshly grated

FOR THE HORSERADISH SAUCE:

1 large cooking apple

100g/4oz button mushrooms

1 tbsp wine vinegar

2 tsps sugar

2 tbsps freshly grated horseradish

Pinch each of salt and white pepper

125ml/4 fl oz whipping cream

Butter and breadcrumbs for the tin

Preparation time: 30 minutes
Cooking time: 40-50 minutes
Nutritional value:

Analysis per slice, approx:
- 1870kJ/445kcal
- 8g protein
- 14g fat
- 12g carbohydrate

Remove the root ends from the chard, wash the leaves and stems thoroughly in cold water, and strip the leaves off the stems. Shred the leaves. Slit the stems in half lengthways, then slice into small pieces. Bring the salted water to the boil. Blanch the Swiss chard for 3 minutes, turn into a colander, drain well and leave to cool. • Preheat the oven to 200°C/400°F/Gas Mark 6. • Cream the butter and egg yolks. Stir in the quark, cream, flour, semolina, salt and nutmeg.
•Squeeze excess moisture out of the chard, and mix into the creamed mixture. • Grease a 26cm/10-inch springform tin with butter, then line with the breadcrumbs. • Pour the Swiss chard mixture into the tin, and smooth over the top. Mix the fresh breadcrumbs and grated cheese, and spread this mixture on top of the flan. Bake on the lowest shelf of the oven for 40-50 minutes; if the top becomes too brown before it is cooked, cover with some greaseproof paper or aluminium foil. • To make the horseradish sauce, peel and grate the apple. Wash, trim and finely chop the mushrooms. Mix the grated apple with the wine vinegar, sugar, horseradish, mushrooms, salt and pepper. Beat the cream until it is thick, and fold into the sauce.
•Serve the sauce with the hot Swiss chard flan.

Our Tip: This dish can be made with spinach instead of Swiss chard.

Tomato Pizza on a Potato Base

A delicious alternative to pastry

Ingredients for 8 slices:

1kg/2¼lbs floury potatoes
1 tbsp lemon juice
3 eggs
125ml/4 fl oz single cream
4 tbsps dry white wine
1 tsp salt
Pinch of sugar
100g/4oz freshly grated pecorino cheese
1 tsp dried oregano
600g/1lb 6oz beefsteak tomatoes
200g/7oz Mozzarella cheese
2 tbsps olive oil
Oil for the tin

Preparation time: 40 minutes
Cooking time: 50 minutes
Nutritional value:
Analysis per slice, approx:
- 1490kJ/355kcal
- 17g protein
- 21g fat
- 23g carbohydrate

Preheat the oven to 200°C/ 400°F/Gas Mark 6. Peel, wash and grate the potatoes, mix with the lemon juice and drain well in a fine sieve. • Grease a flan tin with oil. • Beat the eggs with the cream, wine, salt, sugar, cheese and crushed oregano. Stir the grated potatoes into the mixture, and turn into the greased tin. • Bake on the middle shelf of the oven for 30 minutes; if necessary, cover with greaseproof paper after 15 minutes to prevent excessive browning. • Wash and dry the tomatoes, remove the stalk ends, and slice. Slice the mozzarella. •Remove the potato base from the oven after 30 minutes, and arrange alternating slices of tomato and cheese on it. Sprinkle the oil over them. • Continue cooking for up to another 20 minutes or until the cheese is brown and bubbling.

Our Tip: If you find the potato base too rich, you can also make this Tomato Pizza on a yeast dough base.

Aubergine Pizza

A festive pizza with fillet of beef

Ingredients for a 30cm/12-inch flan (8 slices):

FOR THE DOUGH:

200g/7oz flour

15g/½oz fresh yeast or 8g/¼oz dried yeast

125ml/4 fl oz lukewarm water

1 tbsp olive oil • ½ tsp salt

FOR THE FILLING:

300g/10oz fillet of beef

2 tbsps olive oil

1 tsp fines herbes

2 cloves garlic

600g/1¼lbs aubergines

300g/10oz tomatoes

Salt and white pepper

100g/4oz Pecorino cheese, freshly grated

15g/½oz butter

Olive oil for the dish

Preparation time including standing time: 1 hour
Cooking time: 30 minutes
Nutritional value:

Analysis per slice, approx:
• 1090kJ/260kcal • 15g protein
• 11g fat • 25g carbohydrate

Make a yeast dough with the ingredients following the instructions given for the Onion Flan. • Cut the fillet of beef into strips 1cm/½ inch wide, and marinate in the olive oil with the herbs in a covered dish for 20 minutes. • Peel, chop and crush the cloves of garlic. Slice the aubergines and tomatoes. • Preheat the oven to 200°C/ 400°F/Gas Mark 6. Grease a 30cm/12-inch flan tin. • Roll out the yeast dough and use it to line the tin, raising the sides to form a shallow rim. • Arrange the strips of beef and the sliced aubergines and tomatoes on the pizza base. Sprinkle salt, pepper and crushed garlic on top, and sprinkle with the oil in which the meat has marinated. Scatter the cheese over the pizza and dot with butter. • Bake in the oven for 30 minutes.

Artichoke Pizza

At its best when made with very young artichokes

Ingredients for a 30cm/12-inch flan tin (8 slices):

FOR THE DOUGH:

200g/7oz flour

15g/½oz fresh yeast or 8g/¼oz dried yeast

125ml/4 fl oz lukewarm water

1 tbsp olive oil

Pinch of salt

FOR THE FILLING:

300g/10oz canned tuna

1 small clove garlic

½ tsp salt

1 tbsp olive oil

1 tsp dried thyme

¼ tsp white pepper

16 artichoke hearts

2 tbsps small capers

5 tbsps freshly grated Parmesan

2 egg yolks

3 tbsps crème fraîche

Olive oil to grease the tin

Preparation time including standing time: 1 hour
Cooking time: 30 minutes
Nutritional value:

Analysis per slice, approx:
• 1325kJ/315kcal • 16g protein
• 15g fat • 29g carbohydrate

Preheat the oven to 200°C/ 400°F/Gas Mark 6. Make a yeast dough with the ingredients, following the instructions given for the Onion Flan . • Drain the tuna and break into pieces. Peel and finely chop the garlic, sprinkle salt over it and crush it. Mix it with the olive oil, dried thyme and pepper and pour this over the tuna. Cut the artichoke hearts into quarters. • Grease the dish with oil. • Roll out the dough into a circle and use it to line a 30cm/12-inch flan tin, raising the sides to form a shallow rim. Arrange the artichoke hearts over it, and scatter the capers and pieces of tuna on top. Combine the cheese, egg yolks and crème fraîche, and pour over the dish. • Bake for 30 minutes.

There is More Than One Way of Making a Quiche!

The popularity of quiche is reflected in the variety of fillings on offer

Courgette Quiche
Illustrated on the left

Quantities for a 30cm/12-inch quiche (8 slices):

FOR THE DOUGH:

250g/8oz rye flour

1 egg yolk

100g/4oz vegetable margarine

1 tsp salt

2-4 tbsps water

FOR THE FILLING:

800g/1¾lbs courgettes

2 cloves garlic

2 large onions

2 tbsps olive oil

2 tbsps chopped watercress

4 tbsps chopped chervil

3 eggs

100g/4oz crème fraîche

100g/4oz cracked rye

50g/2oz vegetable margarine

Preparation time: 20 minutes
Cooking time: 40 minutes

Nutritional value:
Analysis per slice, approx:
- 1785kJ/425kcal
- 11g protein
- 26g fat
- 36g carbohydrate

Preheat the oven to 200°C/400°F/Gas Mark 6. • Quickly work the pastry ingredients into a shortcrust dough, roll it out and line the base and sides of a 30cm/12-inch flan tin. • Bake blind for 15 minutes. • Wash and thinly slice the courgettes. Peel and chop the garlic and onions. • Heat the olive oil. Fry the chopped garlic and onion until transparent. Add the sliced courgettes and sauté for about 5 minutes, then mix in the herbs. • Arrange the vegetables in the pastry base. Mix the eggs and crème fraîche and pour over the vegetable mixture. Sprinkle with the rye and top with dabs of margarine. • Cook the quiche for another 25 minutes.

Chicory Quiche
Illustrated on the right

Ingredients for a 28cm/11inch quich (8 slices):

FOR THE PASTRY:

250g/8oz wholewheat flour

1 egg yolk

1 tsp salt

100g/4oz vegetable margarine

2-4 tbsps water

FOR THE FILLING:

800g/1¾lbs chicory

1 red pepper

2 tbsps lemon juice

1 tsp maple or syrup

2 tbsps chopped parsley

2 eggs

1 tsp salt

125ml/4 fl oz sour cream

5 tbsps Emmental cheese, freshly grated

25g/1oz vegetable margarine

Preparation time: 20 minutes
Cooking time: 40-45 minutes
Nutritional value:
Analysis per slice, approx:
- 1280kJ/305kcal
- 9g protein
- 19g fat
- 24g carbohydrate

Preheat the oven to 200°C/400°F/Gas Mark 6. • Quickly work the pastry ingredients into a shortcrust dough, roll it out and line the base and sides of a 30cm/12-inch flan tin. • Bake blind in the oven for 15 minutes. • Meanwhile shred the chicory. Prepare the pepper, dice it and mix with the chicory. Fold in the lemon juice, syrup and parsley. • Beat the eggs with the salt and sour cream, then stir in the cheese. • Place the vegetables in the pre-baked pastry crust, pour the egg and cream mixture over, and top with dabs of margarine. • Bake the quiche for another 25-30 minutes.

Asparagus Quiche

Particularly attractive with green asparagus spears

Quantities for a 30cm/12-inch quiche (8 slices):
750g/1lb 11oz asparagus
2l/3½ pints water
1 tsp salt
1 cube sugar
250g/8oz wholewheat flour
1 egg yolk
½ tsp salt
100g/4oz vegetable margarine
2-4 tbsps cold water
2 eggs
125ml/4 fl oz single cream
4 tbsps freshly grated Jarlsberg cheese

Preparation time: 30 minutes
Cooking time: 30 minutes
Nutritional value:
Analysis per slice, approx:
• 1300kJ/310kcal
• 10g protein
• 20g fat
• 25g carbohydrate

Thinly peel the bottom part of the asparagus stems, cut off the dry woody ends, and wash. Add the salt and cube of sugar to the water, and bring to the boil. Divide the asparagus into four bundles tied together with kitchen thread, place in the boiling water, and boil for about 10 minutes. • To make the shortcrust pastry, sieve the flour onto a work surface, and quickly knead in the egg yolk, salt, margarine and sufficient water to produce a pliable dough. • Preheat the oven to 200°C/400°F/Gas Mark 6. • Roll out the pastry and line the bottom and sides of a 30cm/12-inch flan tin. • Drain the asparagus on a tea-towel, cut into 5cm/2-inch lengths, and arrange on the pastry. • Beat the eggs, cream and cheese together and pour over the asparagus. • Bake the quiche on the middle shelf of the oven for 30 minutes.

Broccoli Quiche

The smoked pork makes this quiche particularly delicious

Ingredients for a 30cm/12-inch Quiche (8 slices):
750g/1lb 11oz broccoli
2l/3½ pints water
1 tsp salt
250g/8oz flour
1 egg yolk
½ tsp salt
50g/2oz butter
2-4 tbsps cold water
200g/7oz smoked loin of pork
2 eggs
A pinch of salt
100g/4oz crème fraîche
1 tsp chopped basil

Preparation time: 35 minutes
Cooking time: 30 minutes
Nutritional value:
Analysis per slice, approx:
• 1115kJ/265kcal
• 14g protein
• 13g fat
• 23g carbohydrate

Clean and trim the broccoli, remove the hard stems and wash the florets. Bring the salted water to the boil and blanch the broccoli florets for 7 minutes. Then drain in a colander and leave to cool. • Preheat the oven to 200°C/400°F/Gas Mark 6. • Make a shortcrust pastry with the flour, egg yolk, salt, butter and water. Line the base and sides of a 30cm/12-inch springform tin with the pastry. Cut the pork into small cubes and scatter over the base. • Arrange the drained broccoli on the pastry. Beat the eggs, salt and crème fraîche together. Stir in the basil, and pour this custard over the broccoli. • Bake the quiche on the middle shelf of the oven for 30 minutes.

Vegetables from A to Z

The following pages reveal yet again the range and diversity of vegetables available. There is a short description of each type, its special properties, suggestions as to which other foods combine well with it and advice on appropriate seasonings and combinations with other foods. Seasonability and storage advice are also given.

It has already been pointed out how valuable vegetables are for a healthy diet. If you study the nutritional data on the various varieties in these descriptions, you will soon realise that vegetables are relatively low in calories but rich in the various nutrients. So you really can eat your fill of vegetables. Above all, you should eat a different variety every day, or better still, eat meals containing a number of different vegetables. This will ensure that you absorb as many different Nutrients as possible.

If you want to or have to keep to a low-salt diet, there is always an indication as to whether a particular variety of vegetable has an especially low sodium content. In any case, you are far better off using herbs for seasoning, allowing the individual flavours of the vegetables to be properly savoured.

Artichokes (Globe)

Artichokes are the buds of a type of thistle; they have a pleasantly aromatic, tart flavour. Early varieties often have purple leaves while later ones tend to be green, but there is virtually no difference in flavour. If the artichokes are very young and small you can eat the whole leaves, but the top third must be cut off when they are larger as the tips become too tough and fibrous. Artichoke hearts are served as a delicacy, either stewed or pickled and eaten cold or baked in the oven, and frequently with a filling.

In season: March to May and October to December.

Nutritional value: rich in fibre, potassium, phosphorus, magnesium, iron and vitamin B_1; also contain protein, fat, carbohydrate, sodium, calcium, vitamins A, B_2, niacin and C. About 230kJ/55kcal per 100g/4oz of the edible part.

Advice on buying: Only buy artichokes with a tight head and succulent, fleshy leaves; select smaller artichokes if there is a choice.

How to store: Keep in the salad compartment of your refrigerator, wrapped in a damp cloth, for up to 3 days.

Preparation and use: Do not cook artichokes in aluminium saucepans; they turn very dark and take on the taste of the metal. Artichokes should be cooked in boiling water until the bottoms are tender, and served with a herb sauce or vinaigrette. You scrape the fleshy part of the artichoke off the leaves with your teeth. Larger artichokes can be filled with mincemeat- or crabmeat-and-rice stuffing and baked. Before stuffing, remove the fibrous part of the flower, which is called the choke, as well as the smaller inside leaves. These leaves can be chopped up and added to the stuffing. The best seasoning for artichokes is lemon juice.

Asparagus

On the Continent, white asparagus is the most popular. The spears are grown in the dark and cut just as they begin to emerge from the ground. French asparagus has purple tips. In Britain, green asparagus is more popular. It has a stronger flavour and is richer in minerals and vitamins as it ripens in the daylight. Wild asparagus is smaller and thinner and is called sprue. For a classic meal of asparagus choose evenly sized, medium-thick spears. When serving it as a salad, soup or side-dish, buy the cheaper thin spears.

In season: April to June.

Nutritional value: rich in fibre, fluorine, vitamins E, B_1, B_2, folic acid, pantothenic acid and vitamin C; also contains protein, fat, carbohydrate, potassium, calcium, phosphorus, iron, vitamins A, K and niacin; low in sodium. About 105kJ/25kcal per 100g/4oz of the edible part.

Advice on buying: look for cut ends that are not dried up; buy medium-thick spears rather than extra-large ones.

How to store: asparagus picked the same day tastes best. If it has to be stored, keep it for no more than 24 hours in the salad compartment of your refrigerator, wrapped in a damp cloth.

Preparation and use: for cocktail snacks and elegant vegetable dishes, soups and decorations use only the tips, reserving the stems for another purpose. Asparagus has a delicate aroma of its own, so it is best to season it very discreetly. You need add only salt and $\frac{1}{2}$ tsp sugar and a knob of butter to the water in which it is boiled. Serve asparagus with melted butter poured over it, with breadcrumbs fried in butter, sauce hollandaise, raw or cooked ham, steak, thin, crispy pancakes or new potatoes.

Aubergines

Fully ripe aubergines - also known as eggplants - generally have a deep purple skin and weigh between 250g/8oz and 800g/1 $\frac{3}{4}$lbs. The tiny seeds embedded in the whitish flesh and the thin skin can be eaten. Varieties imported from Africa are smaller and the skins are white, white streaked with purple or even yellow. Aubergines have a distinctive but pleasant bitter flavour, unless presoaked to leach out the bitterness. They have the advantage of being adaptable and can be made to taste like meat or even fish.

In season: May to October.

Nutritional value: rich in fibre and folic acid; also contain protein, fat, carbohydrate, potassium, calcium, phosphorus, magnesium, iron, vitamins A, B_1, B_2, niacin and C; especially low in sodium. About 105kJ/25kcal per 100g/4oz

Artichokes

Aubergine

Avocados

of the edible part.

Advice on buying: choose aubergines with a smooth, shiny skin; they should be quite firm if pressed, even when ripe. Soft aubergines with wrinkled skin have unpleasantly spongy flesh.

How to store: keep ripe aubergines for up to 3 days in the salad compartment of your refrigerator; under-ripe ones will continue to ripen at room temperature.

Preparation and use: taste the raw aubergine - if it is not too bitter, prepare according to the recipe. If you want to reduce the bitterness, cut the unpeeled aubergine lengthways into fairly thick slices, sprinkle with salt and leave for 15 minutes to draw out the bitter substances. Then rinse the slices in cold water, pat dry and proceed according to the recipe. Aubergines taste good combined with peppers, tomatoes and courgettes; they also lend themselves to recipes using mincemeat. Aubergines can be boiled, fried, baked or steamed. Garlic, paprika, fresh mint, rosemary, lemon juice and onions are suitable seasonings.

Avocados

Avocados are pear-shaped (hence the name 'avocado pear') and have a shiny, leathery, grainy skin which may be dark green, blackish green or deep purple. The flesh surrounding the stone is soft and creamy, and only acquires its delicate, nutty aroma when completely ripe.

In season: all year round.
Nutritional value: rich in fat, fibre, potassium, vitamins E and B_6; also contain protein, carbohydrate, calcium, phosphorus, iron, vitamins A, B_1, and B_2, niacin, pantothenic acid,

and vitamin C; low in sodium. About 985kJ/235kcal per 100g/4oz of the edible part.

Advice on buying: the colour of the skin is no guide to the quality of the avocado. Ripe avocados give slightly at the stalk end when pressed.

How to store: If they are ripe, try to eat them immediately; let under-ripe fruit ripen for 3 to 4 days at room temperature. Do not store in the refrigerator - after being chilled in transit they cannot withstand any further cold.

Preparation and use: avocados can be used for soups, satisfying cocktail snacks and salads, and even in desserts. Their delicate individual flavour goes equally well with savoury seasoning and sweeteners. To make an hors d'oeuvre cut the fruit in half, remove the stone and serve with salad dressing or vinaigrette. Alternatively, scoop out the flesh, chop it up and mix it with shrimps or prawns, anchovy fillets or mixed pickles. Serve in the avocado skin. Anchovy paste, cayenne, parsley, green and white pepper and lemon juice make suitable seasonings.

Beans

Broad Beans
The green pods of broad beans cannot be eaten as they are too coarse and fibrous. The kidney-shaped beans are hulled while they are still tender but relatively large and used as a vegetable. Broad beans contain phasein which makes them indigestible when raw. They therefore need thorough cooking.

In season: July to September.
Nutritional value: except for

calorific value, the same as for dried beans.
About 525kJ/125kcal per 100g/4oz of the edible part.

Advice on buying: shelled broad beans are generally available only frozen or tinned. Fresh ones have only a short season and are bought in their pods. As with green beans, look for dark green, firm pods, and try not to buy any that are damaged, as the beans may already have fallen out of the pod. Remember when you are buying fresh broad beans that you will throw away 35-40% of the weight.

How to store: can be kept for 2 days in the salad compartment of your refrigerator loosely wrapped in paper.

Preparation and use: hull broad beans before you cook them. Cook in a small amount of salted water for up to about 20 minutes until tender, and serve with melted butter or in a tomato sauce (the vegetable water can be used in the sauce). Broad beans taste good with roast gammon, tomatoes and rissoles. Savory, curry powder, dill, parsley and white pepper are suitable seasonings.

Dried Beans
These are the dried seeds of green beans. There are many varieties of bean, and a correspondingly large variety of the dried ones are available. Most beans contain trace elements which are potentially

harmful to health when raw, and so need thorough soaking and cooking. Always discard the soaking water and do not use it for cooking.

Black-eyed beans, also known as black-eyed peas, are small creamy beans with dark ovals on the inside curve, are less widely available; they are as tender as haricot beans, but not so liable to disintegrate during cooking.

Red kidney beans tend to be used particularly for recipes originating from North America such as chile con carne and red beans and rice. They have a pleasant consistency, keep their shape when cooked and are good in slow-cooking stews.

Black beans are small and thin and long and have an especially fine flavour. They are used in Caribbean and South American dishes and to make purées.

Haricot beans. The most widely used beans in European cooking are the small longish white beans with a particularly thin skin known as haricot beans. They are mild in flavour but disintegrate easily when cooked. They are thus useful for thickening soups and casseroles.

Lima beans and the small cylindrical **canellini bean** are also white and can be served as a vegetable or in salads.

Dried runner beans with black spots also collapse quickly during cooking, and are therefore best used in purées.

Cauliflower

Sweet potatoes

Broad beans

Vegetables from A to Z

Flageolet beans are a delicate, pale green colour. These French beans are expensive and should be used with a delicate sauce which does not mask their flavour.

Navy beans are the beans used in baked beans. They are a white, North American variety also called great northern beans.

In season: throughout the year.

Nutritional value: rich in protein, carbohydrate, roughage, potassium, magnesium, iron, vitamins E, B_1 and folic acid; also contain fat, calcium, phosphorus, fluorine, vitamins A, B_2, niacin and vitamin C; low in sodium. About 1365kJ/325kcal per 100g/4oz of the edible part.

Advice on buying: dried beans should not be stored for more than one year after being harvested. When buying, look at the 'best before' date on the packet or box. Examine beans sold loose for dirt and broken or damaged beans. Beans that have been stored for too long can be recognized by their dull, wrinkled skins.

How to store: keep in as cool, dark and airy a place as possible for no more than 6 months, since a long time may have elapsed between harvesting and their appearance in the shops.

Preparation and use: wash dried beans in a bowl of cold water, picking them over as you do so; bad beans will rise to the top and can easily be removed. Then soak for 12 hours or overnight in water that has been boiled and cooled. Cook without salt for between 1 and 2 hours depending on the variety. Only add salt after beans are cooked as salt prevents them from becoming truly tender. The advice that bicarbonate of soda should be added to vegetables during cooking is old-fashioned. Although it does shorten the cooking time and improve the colour, bicarbonate of soda is known to destroy vitamins and flavour. You can shorten the cooking time by about a third by using a pressure cooker. Dried beans taste good with carrots, peppers, tomatoes and onions, as well as with mutton, lamb, beef, pork, roast gammon or sausages. Savory, cayenne pepper, ginger, oregano, paprika, white pepper, sage, and thyme are suitable seasonings.

Green Beans

These are the young, fleshy pods with the seeds ripening inside. As long as the seeds are small and tender, the whole bean is used. Runner beans and the low-growing bush or dwarf beans produce flat-podded beans which are less succulent than the round-podded, fleshy French or string variety, though they belong to the same group. Yellowy wax beans and delicate varieties of French bean, some no thicker than a knitting-needle, belong to the latter category, as do the winged beans which can be found in Indian greengrocers. Most bean varieties no longer require stringing, the exception being runner beans. Green beans should not be eaten raw as they contain a toxin called phasein which can only be eliminated through cooking.

In season: June to September.

Nutritional value: rich in fibre, magnesium, vitamins K and B_6, folic acid and vitamin C; also contain protein, fat, carbohydrate, potassium, calcium, phosphorus, iron, iodine, fluorine, vitamins A, E, B_1, B_2 and niacin; especially low in sodium. About 145kJ/35kcal per 100g/4oz of the edible part.

Advice on buying: only buy firm, bright green or yellow pods; avoid those that are are limp and spotted with brown. Really fresh beans are stiff and can be snapped in half with an audible crack.

How to store: can be kept for 2 days in the salad compartment of your refrigerator loosely wrapped in paper.

Preparation and use: check all beans to see that they are really stringless, and if not string them. Flat-podded beans can be cut slantwise or shredded after they have been washed; large ones should be broken into lengths, while small ones can be left whole. Green beans should be boiled in salted water for a minimum of 10 minutes – or longer, depending on the variety and how thick they are – rinsed in cold water, drained, and finished as desired. Alternatively, beans can be quickly sautéed in fat with a chopped onion over high heat; water or stock is then added, and the cooking should continue on a low heat until done. This gives them a particularly brilliant green colour. Beans taste good tossed in butter, combined with beef, pork, ham, fried diced bacon, potatoes, carrots, tomatoes and onions. Green beans are often seasoned with mixed herbs, but garlic, savory, oregano, parsley, sage and thyme are also possible.

Beetroot

Beetroot are brownish-red on the outside with purple-red flesh. They are juicy with a delicate distinctive flavour. They can be eaten cooked in salads and soups or used for their juice which is also used as a natural colouring.

In season: September to February.

Nutritional value: rich in fibre, potassium and folic acid; also contains protein, fat, carbohydrate, sodium, calcium, phosphorus, iron, vitamins A, B_1 and B_2, niacin and vitamin C. About 190kJ/45kcal per 100g/4oz of the edible part.

Advice on buying: buy small, plump, raw beetroot with undamaged skins; the larger and older beetroot are, the more cellulose they contain, and consequently the longer they take to cook. Beetroot are also sold ready-cooked for use in salads.

How to store: keep wrapped in paper for up to 1 week in the salad compartment of the refrigerator.

Preparation and use: Either

Green beans

Broccoli

Dried beans

steam or boil beetroot, unpeeled, for 1-2 hours until tender, depending on their size, then peel and use as you wish. Remember that beetroot juice is a powerful red dye and it is difficult to get it off your hands (you may prefer to wear rubber gloves when peeling, grating or cutting beetroot) and even harder to get it out of fabric. Beetroot tastes good with onions, and goes well with freshly-grated root ginger, ground coriander, caraway seeds, grated horseradish, crushed mustard seeds and lemon.

Broccoli

Broccoli with its dark green or sometimes purple-green dense, curled florets is related to cauliflower, and is slightly reminiscent of asparagus in flavour. With its delicate aroma and tender consistency it has for years been a favourite winter vegetable for special occasions. The very dense variety is known as calabrese and is grown largely in the Channel Islands.

In season: November to March
Nutritional value: rich in fibre, potassium, calcium, magnesium, vitamins A, K, B_2, B_6, folic acid, pantothenic acid and vitamin C ; also contains protein, fat, carbohydrate, phosphorus, vitamin B_1 and niacin; very low in sodium. About 145kJ/35kcal per 100g/4oz of the edible part.
Advice on buying: only buy dark green heads with stiff leaves, stems and bracts. Flabby flowers

and yellow bracts indicate that the broccoli has been stored too long.
How to store: wrap in airtight clingfilm or foil and keep in the salad compartment of your refrigerator for up to 2 days.
Preparation and use: while broccoli cannot be eaten raw, it cooks very quickly. Remove the bracts from the florets, wash in several changes of water, thinly peel the stalks from top to bottom as for asparagus, and make an X-shaped incision in the bottom. Or you can cut off the stems and cook them for 6 minutes on their own, then add the florets and cook together for another 6 minutes. Broccoli should be boiled for between 10 and 15 minutes in salted water, drained, then served with melted butter, hollandaise sauce or a cream sauce. It combines well with mushrooms, flaked almonds, carrots, asparagus and tomatoes. Garlic, nutmeg, parsley, pepper, allspice and lemon juice are suitable seasonings.

Brussels Sprouts

These are actually a miniature variety of cabbage, and a typical winter vegetable. The flavour is improved by the first frosts; thus the stems from which they actually sprout are the best storage place for them during the winter months.
In season: September to February.
Nutritional value: rich in fibre, potassium, magnesium, iron,

vitamins K, B2 and B6, folic acid and vitamin C ; also contain protein, fat, carbohydrate, calcium, phosphorus, iodine, vitamins A, B1 and niacin; low in sodium. About 210kJ/50kcal per 100g/4oz of the edible part.
Advice on buying: select Brussels sprouts that are as small as possible with tightly-closed heads and dark green leaves; limp, yellowing outer leaves suggest that the vegetables have been stored in too warm a place for too long.
How to store: in the salad compartment of your refrigerator wrapped in paper for up to 2 days.
Preparation and use: if necessary, remove the outer leaves, trim the stalks and make a crossways incision in the ends. Wash and cook gently in a small amount of water for up to 10-15 minutes depending on size. Brussels sprouts taste good mixed with chestnuts, with hamburgers, ham or bacon, baked in the oven with cheese or in a cream sauce. Of course, they are traditional with the Christmas turkey. A bay leaf, nutmeg, white pepper, parsley, sage and lemon juice are suitable seasonings.

Cardoon

Cardoons, which are something of

a rarity in the UK, are popular on the Continent. They belong to the thistle family, and in flavour resemble artichokes, to which they are related. They look like silver-grey celery stalks. Only the broad, thick, fleshy stalks of the plant are used and they are always cooked.
In season: June to October.
Nutritional value: precise data not available. About 105kJ/25kcal per 100g/4oz of the edible part.
Advice on buying: only buy heads with light, fleshy stems; choose smaller heads if available. Expect to throw away about 50% of what you buy.
How to store: keep for up to 2 days in the salad compartment of the refrigerator wrapped in a damp cloth (re-wet the cloth if it dries).
Preparation and use: discard the leaves, hollow ends and edges of the cardoon stalks. Pull off the long fibres as you would for rhubarb, and sprinkle immediately with lemon juice to prevent discolouration. Cut the cardoon into pieces, cook gently in a small amount of water for about 20 minutes, and serve in a cream sauce. Cardoons also taste good with ham or mincemeat, or baked in the oven with cheese. Tarragon, mace and lemon juice are suitable as seasonings.

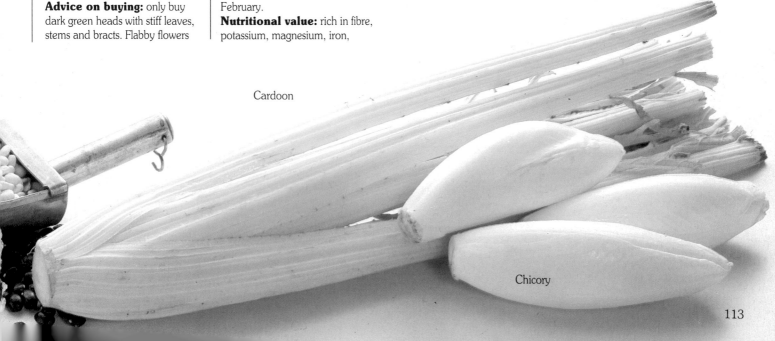

Cardoon

Chicory

Vegetables from A to Z

Carrots

Carrots come in many shapes and sizes, though baby carrots are hard to find in the shops as they are mainly used by the canning industry. Summer and autumn carrots have long roots with pointed or stumpy ends, and they vary in thickness.

In season: May to September. Imported or stored carrots are available in the winter months.

Nutritional value: rich in fibre, potassium and vitamin A; also contain protein, fat, carbohydrate, sodium, calcium, phosphorus, magnesium, iron, iodine, fluorine, vitamins K, B_1 and B_2, niacin and vitamin C.
About 170kJ/40kcal per 100g/4oz of the edible part.

Advice on buying: when buying bunches of summer carrots, look for green leaves, and later in the year look for undamaged roots with no signs of rot.

How to store: eat summer carrots the day you buy them if possible, as they soon lose their moisture and go limp. Store thicker autumn carrots in a dark airy place protected from drying out, i.e. wrapped in paper, for up to a week. If you have a large quantity, store them in a cool shed or cellar in a box containing a mixture of sand and soil for up to 2 months.

Preparation and use: scrub young carrots thoroughly under cold running water. Do not scrape them, and depending on their size leave whole or slice lengthways; scrape or peel older carrots, wash, then shred, dice or slice them. If the carrots are very thick you may have to cut out the yellowish core, which tends to be green near the root. Carrots are also digestible and particularly tasty when eaten raw. They combine well with peas, green beans, leeks, onions, white cabbage and celery; raw, they go well with apples, oranges, celery and nuts. Aniseed, fennel seeds, ginger, white pepper, allspice, parsley, mint, honey, maple syrup and a little fat to help utilise the vitamin A are good seasonings for carrots.

Cauliflower

Cauliflower is the outsized, unopened flower of the cabbage plant. This easily digestible vegetable can be used to make soups, salads and vegetable dishes.

In season: June to November.

Nutritional value: rich in fibre; potassium, vitamins K and B_6, folic acid, pantothenic acid and vitamin C ; also contains protein, fat, carbohydrate, calcium, phosphorus, magnesium, iron, iodine, vitamins A, B_1, B_2, and niacin; especially low in sodium.
About 105kJ/25kcal per 100g/4oz of the edible part.

Advice on buying: look for tightly packed, creamy white florets with no dark blemishes.

How to store: keep loosely wrapped in paper for up to 3 days in the salad compartment of your refrigerator.

Preparation and use: it is best to steam cauliflower in a colander or vegetable steamer over boiling water, or boil it in water with no added salt - do not overcook; add salt after it is cooked as it can cause the florets to discolour. Cauliflower is particularly mild in flavour if it is cooked in a mixture of milk and water (equal parts). When cauliflower is removed from the pot after cooking cooked, it should not fall apart. If it is broken up into florets, it can also be cooked by the conservative cooking method, i.e., with a very small amount of water. Cauliflower tastes good with breadcrumbs fried in butter, and combined with ham or mildly-seasoned minced meat. Cayenne, chervil, nutmeg, parsley, white pepper, chives and celery salt may be used to season it.

Celeriac

The young roots which are a light earthy colour, about the size of a fist, and still bear their thin stems and green leaves are seldom found in this country. More widely available are fully-grown roots which are dark brown and knobbly and weigh up to 1kg/2¼lbs. Celeriac is often used as a seasoning because of its powerful flavour.

In season: October to March.

Nutritional value: rich in fibre, potassium, vitamins E and B_6; also contains protein, fat, carbohydrate, sodium, calcium, phosphorus, magnesium, iron, iodine, fluorine, vitamins A, K, B_1, B_2, niacin and vitamin C.
About 170kJ/40kcal per 100g/4oz of the edible part.

Advice on buying: Large roots should be heavy – spongy areas are often concealed inside. When choosing young roots look for fresh leaves.

How to store: keep in the salad compartment of your refrigerator for up to 2 weeks; cut celeriac should be wrapped tightly in foil and kept up to 1 week. You can store your winter supply covered in sand in a cool dark shed or cellar.

Preparation and use: celeriac can be steamed or boiled in its skin (after being thoroughly scrubbed) for between 40 minutes and 1 hour depending on size. Alternatively, it can be peeled, diced or sliced, then cooked gently in a little water for 20-30 minutes. Scatter the tender green leaves, some of them chopped, over the cooked vegetable. Celeriac may also be used raw, grated or cut into julienne strips. It combines well with carrots, leeks and potatoes, or raw with apples, pineapple, carrots and nuts. Celery leaves, lovage, parsley, thyme, lemon juice and vinegar may be used as seasoning.

Celery

Celery is blanched by heaping up earth round it while it is growing to keep it from turning green. Slender, tender sticks are best eaten raw, thicker ones should be used for cooking.

In season: October to March.

Nutritional value: rich in fibre, potassium and calcium; also

Chinese leaves

Garden peas

Dried peas

contains protein, fat, carbohydrate, sodium, phosphorus, magnesium, iron, vitamins A, B₁, B₂, niacin and vitamin C.

About 85kJ/20kcal per 100g/4oz of the edible part.

Advice on buying: look for pale-green, springy, fleshy stems and fresh green leaves.

How to store: washed and wrapped in a damp cloth, it will keep in the salad compartment of your refrigerator for 3 days.

Preparation and use: add the chopped green leaves to cooked food. Pull the long fibres off thick sticks of celery as you would with rhubarb. Celery has a powerful flavour of its own, so it does not need any special seasoning.

Chicory

Long heads of chicory with tightly overlapping pale yellow leaves and tender green tips are grown in the dark, which gives them their light colour and makes the leaves so tender in consistency. The flavour of the crisp leaves is slightly bitter.

In season: November to March.

Nutritional value: rich in fibre, magnesium, vitamin A and folic acid; also contains protein, fat, carbohydrate, potassium, calcium, phosphorus, iron, vitamins B₁, B₂, niacin and vitamin C; especially low in sodium.

About 65kJ/15kcal per 100g/4oz of the edible part.

Advice on buying: look for heads that are tightly closed right up to the tips of the leaves. The outside leaves should never have

brown, rotten areas.

How to store: wrapped in several layers of paper in the salad compartment of the refrigerator for up to 4 days.

Preparation and use: chicory is best if used in salads where it is combined with sweet or sour fruit, nuts, various types of lettuce, carrots, peppers and tomatoes. Cooked chicory is good in soups, and the heads may be cut in half, wrapped in ham and cheese and cooked in lightly browned butter. To reduce the bitterness, cut off part of the root end, then remove a 2cm/³/₄-inch wedge from what remains of the root end as most of the bitter substances are concentrated there. Curry powder, dill, ginger, nutmeg, paprika, parsley, white pepper and lemon juice may be used to season.

Chinese Leaves

Chinese leaves are easy to digest, tender and mild-flavoured. They are equally useful in salads and as a cooked vegetable. The longish heads range in colour from yellowish-green to light green. They weigh up to 1kg/2¼lbs.

In season: October to March.

Nutritional value: rich in fibre, folic acid and vitamin C ; also contain protein, fat, carbohydrate, potassium, calcium, phosphorus, magnesium, iron, fluorine, vitamins A, B₁, B₂ and niacin; especially low in sodium.

About 65kJ/15kcal per 100g/4oz of the edible part.

Advice on buying: choose heads that are as tightly closed as possible with fresh, stiff leaves; leaves that are turning brown suggest that the leaves have been badly stored.

How to store: wrapped in airtight foil in the salad compartment of your refrigerator for 10 days.

Preparation and use: shredded Chinese leaves taste good in a salad with grated apple or carrots, mandarins, chopped nuts, lamb's lettuce and celery. As a cooked vegetable they go well with peas, spring onions, leeks, carrots and mushrooms. Stuffed Chinese leaves with a well-seasoned mincemeat filling are very delicious. Cooked conservatively (i.e. with very little water) Chinese leaves go well with tomato sauce. Basil, ginger, parsley, mint, a hint of allspice and mild soya sauce can all be used to season them.

Courgettes

Courgettes which are also known by their Italian name, zucchini, are miniature marrows, the size of small cucumbers; they are 10-30cm/4-12inches in length, with a skin colour ranging from light to dark green, sometimes with yellow stripes. The small seeds contained

in the pale flesh and the skin can be eaten.

In season: May to October.

Nutritional value: rich in fibre; also contain protein, fat, carbohydrate, potassium, calcium, phosphorus, vitamins A, B₁, B₂, niacin and vitamin C; especially low in sodium.

About 125kJ/30kcal per 100g/4oz of the edible part.

Advice on buying: avoid any with soft skins that can easily be scratched with your finger-nail. Choose only firm courgettes which do not yield to pressure. Firm, small ones have more flavour, if they are available.

How to store: wrapped loosely in paper in the salad compartment of the refrigerator for up to 5 days.

Preparation and use: for best results slice unpeeled courgettes and fry or grill them. Alternatively, cut them in half lengthways, scoop out a hollow and stuff with

Kale

Fennel

115

Vegetables from A to Z

chopped meat stuffing or fricasséed chicken, then bake in the oven. Cayenne, dill, garlic, parsley, white pepper, fresh mint and lemon juice can be used as seasoning.

Cress and Watercress

Cress, also known as mustard-and-cress or hot-and-dry, plays a relatively small role in vegetable cookery, as does watercress. However both are excellent garnishes for raw vegetables and cooked vegetable dishes. Cress not only provides important vitamins, it also enhances the flavour of the food. Watercress is puréed and mixed with stock and cream to make watercress soup. Land cress resembles watercress and is a popular vegetable for the garden.
In season: for garden cress, all the year round; for watercress, July to October.
Nutritional value (garden cress): rich in fibre, potassium, calcium, iron, vitamins A and C; also contains protein, fat, carbohydrate, phosphorus, fluorine, vitamins B_1, B_2, and niacin; especially low in sodium. About 190kJ/45kcal per 100g/4oz of the edible part.
Nutritional value

(watercress): rich in fibre, potassium, calcium, iron, vitamins A, B_1, and C; also contains protein, fat, carbohydrate, phosphorus, vitamin B_2 and niacin; especially low in sodium. About 190kJ/45kcal per 100g/4oz of the edible part.
Advice on buying: always look for fresh, dark green leaves.
How to store: cress will keep fresh growing in its box on the kitchen window-sill for 1-2 weeks; water it from time to time. Watercress does not keep for more than a day or two in the refrigerator.
Preparation and use: cut cress with scissors, rinse it thoroughly and drain. Wash watercress thoroughly and chop. The leaves may also be used whole in salads and with vegetables. Cress combines well with citrus segments.

Cucumbers

Long, thin salad cucumbers are available throughout the year, grown under glass or imported from warmer countries. Ridge cucumbers, grown outdoors, have more flavour. The last of the crop can be used in late summer and early autumn for pickling.
In season: June to October.
Nutritional value: rich in fibre; also contains protein, fat, carbohydrate, potassium, calcium, phosphorus, magnesium, iron, iodine, vitamins A, B_1, B_2, niacin and folic acid; low in sodium. About 65kJ/15kcal per 100g/4oz of the edible part.
Advice on buying: look for firm cucumbers with no soft or rotten

parts, and for undamaged, shiny dark green skins. Late ridge cucumbers may have skins that are slightly yellowed, which indicates that they are almost over-ripe, but also particularly full of flavour.
How to store: in the salad compartment of the refrigerator or in a cool, dark place for up to 3 days. If the cucumber has been cut, cover the cut surface with clingfilm, then store for not more than 24 hours in the salad compartment of the refrigerator.
Preparation and use: many cucumbers contain bitter juices that are released from the stalk end, and these are not to everyone's liking. So taste small slices from that end of the washed cucumber, and keep on cutting until the bitterness attenuates. If you peeled the cucumber before doing this, the bitterness could be spread right through the cucumber by the act of peeling, so peel the cucumber and rinse it briefly again. Cucumbers to be used for cooking should be halved lengthways and the seeds scraped out with a spoon; then peel the cucumber, or stuff it unpeeled. Young salad cucumbers that have been grown outdoors are best used unpeeled after careful washing. For cucumber salad, dill is the ideal flavouring, but fennel leaves or salad burnet, lemon

juice, cream, yogurt or crème fraîche go well with cucumber too, as do shrimps. Braised cucumbers are good with a mincemeat stuffing, or sliced and served in a mustard sauce.

Dandelion Leaves

Dandelion leaves are becoming popular again as edible plants. They are often used in mixed green salads, with other wild leaves, such as young nettles and nasturtiums. They can occasionally be found in the shops.
In season: May to September.
Nutritional value: rich in fibre, potassium, calcium, magnesium, iron, vitamins A and B_1; also contain protein, fat, carbohydrate, sodium, phosphorus, vitamin B_2, niacin and vitamin C. About 190kJ/45kcal per 100g/4oz of the edible part.
Advice on buying: if possible select only young, small, clean plants.
How to store: dandelion leaves are best used directly they are picked. If they have to be stored, wash, drain, wrap loosely in foil, and store in the salad

Celeriac

Kohlrabi

Potatoes

Cucumber

116

compartment of your refrigerator for a maximum of 12 hours.

Preparation and use: if you are picking your own dandelion leaves, avoid fields near heavily-used roads and make sure that the grass has not been sprayed with chemicals in the last 3 weeks or so. Young dandelion leaves keep growing in the summer after the grass has been mown, so that there is an opportunity to gather dandelions yourself over a period of several months. For salads, dress dandelion leaves with vinaigrette sauce or a mixture of yogurt and crème fraîche. If using them as a vegetable, prepare and cook dandelion leaves like spinach and serve in a cream sauce. White pepper, crisply fried diced bacon and lemon juice can be used as seasoning.

Fennel

The fennel bulb is the thickened stem of the fennel plant, which has narrow, feathery leaves. It consists of fleshy, whitish-green ribbed stalks. The long green stems that grow out of the bulb are not used, but the leaves are used as a herb. Fennel tastes strongly of aniseed.

In season: October to April.
Nutritional value: rich in fibre and vitamin A; also contains protein, fat and carbohydrate. About 105kJ/25kcal per 100g/4oz of the edible part.

Advice on buying: only buy firm white or pale green bulbs; bulbs with dry brownish outer stalks have been kept for too long.
How to store: for up to 2 days in the salad compartment of the refrigerator. First cut off any green stems and feathery leaves, wash them and the bulb, and wrap in a damp cloth.
Preparation and use: remove the hard ribs from the outer leaves. Immediately you have chopped it up, sprinkle lemon juice over fennel to prevent discoloration. For mixed salads shred or grate it; for use as a vegetable, separate the leaves and cut into slightly smaller pieces. Always add the feathery green leaves raw to the cooked dish. Cook fennel in a small amount of water with a little olive oil. Cooked fennel in cream sauce tastes good with sautéed meat, with poultry and ham, and baked in the oven with cheese. It is especially delicious with fish. Garlic, nutmeg and lemon juice are suitable seasonings.

Jerusalem Artichokes

This is the edible tuber of a species of sunflower, and native to the United States. In appearance Jerusalem artichokes are reminiscent of fresh root ginger or tiny, knobbly potatoes, and in flavour they are a little like globe artichokes and nuts. They are very tender when cooked and their distinctive flavour makes them a useful ingredient in salads and appetisers. Cooked by the conservative method or roasted, they make a tasty vegetable. As the tuber contains the carbohydrate inulin rather than starch, it is particularly suited to diabetics.

In season: November to March.
Nutritional value: rich in carbohydrate, fibre, potassium, magnesium, iron and vitamin B_1; also contains protein, fat, calcium, phosphorus, vitamins A, B_2, niacin and vitamin C; low in sodium. About 335kJ/80kcal per 100g/4oz of the edible part.
Advice on buying: select undamaged tubers that are as small as possible as these are more tender and milder in flavour than the large ones.
How to store: try to use on the day of purchase. Jerusalem artichokes can be successfully stored only if buried in sand in a cool, dark place.
Preparation and use: scrub thoroughly under running water; grate coarsely without peeling for salads, or boil for up to about 20 minutes as for potatoes in their skins. To bring out the distinctive flavour season only with lemon juice, a hint of caraway seed, salt and a little white pepper.

Kale, Curly Kale

This sustaining winter vegetable, a member of the cabbage family, is exceptionally rich in minerals and vitamins. It gets its bitter-sweet flavour through exposure to the frost which converts the starch in the cabbage into sugar. The best known variety of kale has very crinkly leaves; there is a smooth-leaved variety, but it is seldom available commercially.

In season: November to March.
Nutritional value: rich in protein, fibre, potassium, calcium, magnesium, iron, iodine, vitamins A, E, B_2, B_6, folic acid and vitamin C; also fat, carbohydrate, sodium, fluorine, vitamins B_1 and C. About 230kJ/55kcal per 100g/4oz of the edible part.
Advice on buying: look out for leaves that are fleshy and as small as possible; expect to lose 50% of the weight when you discard the stalks.
How to store: wrapped in aluminium foil in the salad compartment of your refrigerator for no more than 1 day.
Preparation and use: remove and discard the stems and any damaged leaves. Wash in several changes of water as earth or sand can cling to the crinkly leaves. Blanch in salted water for 10 minutes, then chop and braise until tender for up to 1 hour. Kale is served with hearty meat dishes, such as sausages, pork chops or spareribs; it goes well with mashed potatoes and onions fried in butter. The slightly acrid flavour is modified if it is served in a creamy sauce. Basil, coriander, nutmeg, black pepper and allspice are suitable seasonings.

Kohlrabi

These bulbs are the thickened stems of the plant. Kohlrabi can have either a pale green or a dark purple skin, but there is no difference in flavour or content between the two varieties. The leaves of the plant have special nutritional value, though they are not often sold commercially. The tender inside leaves should always

Swede

Cress

Vegetables from A to Z

be chopped up raw and added to the cooked dish.

In season: May to October.

Nutritional value: rich in fibre and vitamin C ; also contains protein, fat, carbohydrate, calcium, phosphorus, magnesium, iron, iodine, vitamins A, B_1, B_2 and niacin; especially low in sodium. About 125kJ/30kcal per 100g/4oz of the edible part.

Advice on buying: try to buy medium-sized bulbs with no cracks; look for fresh green leaves.

How to store: in the salad compartment of your refrigerator for 3 days.

Preparation and use: use young kohlrabi raw in salads or with other raw vegetables, stuff larger ones with minced meat or fish. Use it in casseroles, stews or soups. Lovage, nutmeg, parsley, white pepper and salad burnet are good seasonings.

Leeks

Leeks are members of the onion family, but do not form a bulb. Summer leeks have pale green, curved, thin-skinned leaves which turn yellow towards the stem and are white near the root. They are milder in flavour than the acrid winter leek. The stems of winter leeks are thicker, and the dark green top part of the leek can be used only for flavouring. Only the yellow and white parts of the winter leek are used.

In season: summer leeks, May to August; winter leeks, September to April.

Nutritional value (in the white and yellow part of the leek): rich in fibre, calcium, vitamins E, B_6, folic acid and vitamin C; also contain protein, fat, carbohydrate, potassium, phosphorus, magnesium, iron, vitamins A, B_1, B_2 and niacin; especially low in sodium. About 145kJ/35kcal per 100g/4oz of the edible part.

Advice on buying: avoid leeks with yellowish, brown-stained leaves and any sign of rot. Expect to throw away 50% of the weight of winter leeks, about 30% of summer leeks.

How to store: after removing any damaged leaves, wrap in a thick layer of paper and keep in the salad compartment of your refrigerator for up to 3 days; take care that the smell does not taint other food.

Preparation and use: always wash leeks thoroughly, opening the leaves well out, as a lot of sand and earth can lodge between them. Slit winter leeks in half lengthways, cut into pieces and blanch in salted water for 10 minutes, then follows the recipe instructions. Summer leeks can be braised whole. Leeks are nice with carrots, white cabbage, ham, boiled beef, baked in the oven with cheese, and in a cream sauce. Cayenne pepper, tarragon, chervil, garlic, lovage, nutmeg, parsley and thyme are suitable seasonings.

Lentils

Lentils are the dried seeds of a plant related to vetch. Several varieties are available commercially, the largest being 6-7mm/^{1}/3inch in diameter, medium ones 4-6mm/^{1}/4inch, and small split lentils less than 4mm/^{1}/4 inch. There are red lentils (also known as Egyptian lentils), green (Puy) lentils, brown and even black lentils, though black ones are not widely available. Colour is less important in determining the flavour than size. Although large lentils cost more, the small ones taste better as there is proportionately more skin and the flavour is mainly stored in the skins. Freshly harvested lentils are pale green, but once exposed to the light they turn brown, yellowish-brown or brownish-red, though this does not affect the taste or nutritional value.

In season: all year round.

Nutritional value: rich in protein, carbohydrate, fibre, iron and vitamin B_1; also contain fat, potassium, calcium, phosphorus, fluorine, vitamins A, B_2 and niacin; especially low in sodium. About 1385kJ/330kcal per 100g/4oz of the edible part.

Advice on buying: dried, undamaged lentils may be stored for for up to 3 years. If buying them loose, look out for dirt and pests; you can recognize lentils that have been stored too long by their broken, lacklustre appearance. When buying canned meals containing lentils, pay particular attention to the expiry date.

How to store: store for a maximum of 2 years at most in a place that is as dark, cool and as airy as possible – between the time they were harvested and their appearance in the shops 1 or 2 years may already have elapsed.

Preparation and use: dried lentils need not be soaked. Wash in a bowl of water, discarding any bad ones that float to the surface. Discard the soaking water. Like dried peas and beans, lentils should be cooked without salt in fresh water for up to 1 or 1 ^{1}/2 hours. You can reduce the cooking time by two-thirds if you use a pressure cooker. Dried lentils are often served puréed with a joint of beef, steak or venison. They are also casseroled with potatoes, pasta or gnocchi and combined with prunes, leeks, carrots and onions. They may be seasoned with maple syrup, vinegar, tarragon, cloves, paprika, parsley, white pepper, lemon and sugar.

Okra

Also known as bhindi, gumbo or lady's finger, the okra is one of the oldest known African vegetables. Only young okra is good to eat. The pale green, hexagonal pods are covered with a fine down. The small soft seeds inside emit a pale liquid which has binding properties when they are cooked.

In season: October to April.

Nutritional value: rich in fibre, calcium, magnesium, vitamin C;

Pumpkin

Dandelion leaves

Leeks

Lentils

also contain protein, fat, carbohydrate, potassium, phosphorus, iron, vitamins A, B_1, B_2 and niacin.
About 190kJ/45kcal per 100g/4oz of the edible part.

Advice on buying: try to buy okra that is as small as possible, no longer than a finger, with a delicate down; if the skin is prickly it is no longer good to eat.

How to store: wrapped loosely in paper for up to 2 days in the salad compartment of your refrigerator.

Preparation and use: never peel okra - wash it thoroughly, pat dry and cut off the tip and the stalk end. Halve the pods or cut into strips, and cook gently in a small amount of salted water, or with aubergines, sweetcorn and/or tomatoes. Cayenne, chillies, curry powder, ginger, garlic, coriander, cress and lemon juice can be used to season them.

Onions

There are many varieties of onion which vary in size, shape and colour. In flavour they range from sweet and mild to powerfully pungent.

The brown-skinned onion is white inside and has a moderate degree of pungency. This is the most widely used for salads, soups and in dishes containing potatoes, vegetables and meat.

The Spanish onion is extra large, with a paler or even a white skin. It is considered to be milder and is served with a stuffing or as a vegetable in its own right.

The red onion, has a red skin and red edges on the white inner rings. It is also a mild variety and may be served as an accompaniment, boiled using the conservative method, fried, or coated in batter to make fritters. However, the flavour of some red onions is even stronger than that of brown-skinned onions and they should therefore be used sparingly as a seasoning. They are also excellent in salads.

Small white onion really has to be tasted before you decide how to use it. If mild, it can be chopped up and added to a salad, used to garnish meat dishes or grilled.

Spring onions are in fact available throughout the year now, but their flavour is best in spring. The white, spherical swelling and the bright green tubular leaves are chopped up for salads and to garnish vegetable dishes.

Shallots with their mild flavour are used wherever the brown-skinned onion would be rather too powerful, for example for appetisers, salads, sauces and subtle meat dishes. Gently cooked whole, in butter or glazed, shallots make a superb side-dish.

Pearl onions, also known as silver-skin onions, rarely feature at all in vegetable cookery. They are available occasionally for making home-made pickles.

In season: most varieties are available all year round now, but the true seasons are:
brown-skinned onions, all year;
Spanish onions, June to November;
spring onions, April to June.
Nutritional value: rich in fibre;

also contain protein, fat, carbohydrate, potassium, calcium, phosphorus, iron, iodine, fluorine, vitamins A, E, B_1, B_2, niacin and vitamin C; low in sodium.
About 165kJ/40kcal per 100g/4oz of the edible part.

Advice on buying: Only select dry, plump onions with no soft or hollow spots or shoots. With spring onions look for rounded white ends, leaves that are not too long and are crisp and fresh.

How to store: keep spring onions in the salad compartment of your refrigerator for up to 3 days; store all other onions in a cool, dry, airy atmosphere in a dark place. The temperature should not fall below 4°C/40°F.

Preparation and use: remove the papery skin, cut off the root end and any shoots and then prepare according to the recipe. To give colour to meat gravy or stock, do not skin the onions; you can roast halved onions with the cut surface directly on the hot plate (or in an iron frying-pan) to make them release both their colouring and their flavour.

Parsnips

Parsnips have long, pointed, whitish roots. In flavour they are slightly reminiscent of celeriac and celery, but the flavour is rather pungent.

In season: November to February.

Nutritional value: rich in carbohydrate, fibre, potassium, and magnesium; also contain protein, fat, calcium, phosphorus,

iron, vitamins A, B_1, B_2, niacin, folic acid and vitamin C; especially low in sodium.
About 295kJ/70kcal per 100g/4oz of the edible part.

Advice on buying: try to select regular-shaped, small to medium, undamaged roots; outsize ones can be woody and taste bitter.

How to store: in the salad compartment of your refrigerator for up 10 days.

Preparation and use: peel parsnips thinly, cut into dice, sticks or slices and cook for 20-25 minutes. The flavour of parsnips goes well with carrots and potatoes; on their own they taste best in a cream sauce. Aniseed, fennel seeds or fennel leaves, honey, ground coriander and parsley make good seasonings.

Peas

Dried peas and Chick-peas

Dried peas are the mature, dried seeds of the pea plant which have been removed from their pods. Yellow, green and bluish dried peas are available commercially, some with their skins and others without. You can make purées, pease pudding and cream of pea soup from those that are already skinned. If you are using them as a vegetable or for a casserole, the unskinned peas are better as they are more nutritious. When the skin is removed, the peas often fall in

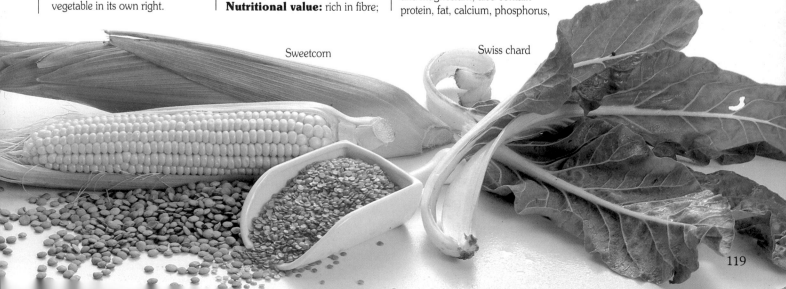

Sweetcorn   Swiss chard

half, and are then sold as split peas which can be used in the same way as other skinned, dried peas. Chick-peas are a little larger, irregular in shape and range from yellow to light brown in colour. Their mild nutty flavour is typical of special dishes from the Mediterranean area, but they can be used for all well-known dishes made with dried peas.

In season: all year round.

Nutritional value: rich in protein, carbohydrate, fibre, magnesium and vitamin B_1; also contain fat, potassium, calcium, phosphorus, iron, vitamins A, B_2, niacin, folic acid and vitamin C; especially low in sodium. About 1450kJ/345kcal per 100g/4oz of the edible part.

Advice on buying: dried peas should not be stored for more than 1 year. Look at the expiry date on the packet or can when you are buying them. Examine those sold loose for dirt and insects. You can recognize dried peas that have been stored too long by their lacklustre, wrinkled skins.

How to store: try to store in a place that is cool, dark and airy for a maximum of 6 months. 6 months may already have elapsed between the time the peas were harvested and their appearance in the shops.

Preparation and use: wash dried peas in a bowl of water, picking them over as you do so; bad ones float to the top and can easily be removed. Then soak them for 12 hours or overnight in water that has been boiled and cooled. Do not cook in the water in which they have soaked but use fresh water, without salt, and boil for 2-3 hours depending on the

variety and type. Chick-peas take about $1^{1}/_{2}$ hours to cook, shelled, dried peas take only 20-30 minutes. Do not salt dried peas until after cooking as the salt prevents them from becoming really soft. The advice that bicarbonate of soda should be added to dried peas during cooking is old-fashioned, although it does shorten the cooking time; bicarbonate of soda is known to destroy vitamins and flavour. You can shorten the cooking time by about two thirds by using a pressure cooker. Dried peas taste good with pork, fried bacon, smoked sausage, and fried onion rings. Mugwort, marjoram, nutmeg, oregano, parsley, black pepper, purslane, chives and lemon balm are suitable seasonings.

Garden peas

Unfortunately the food industry has hijacked this noble vegetable so, although masses of cheap, canned peas are available everywhere, they all have the same insipid flavour. They are generally the large variety from which all the flavour has been removed by over-pasteurisation. Frozen peas are preferable to canned ones both as regards flavour and nutritional value. Buy fresh garden peas whenever they are available. To serve as a vegetable in soups and casseroles, use shelled peas. The fibrous pods are not edible. Marrowfat peas are more angular and sometimes a little wrinkled. The irregular outer surface is no guide to their quality

– marrowfat peas taste slightly sweet and have a very subtle texture. Mangetout, or snow peas, are whole pods. They are used extensively in Chinese cooking. Use them in omelettes, vegetable side-dishes and casseroles.

In season: June to August.

Nutritional value: rich in protein, fibre, potassium, magnesium, iron, vitamins E, K, B_1, B_2, niacin, vitamin B_6, folic acid, pantothenic acid and vitamin C ; also contain fat, carbohydrate, calcium, phosphorus, fluorine and vitamins A; low in sodium. About 335kJ/80kcal per 100g/4oz of the edible part.

Advice on buying: with fresh peas, the pods should account for half of the weight, so if you are not using the whole pods you can expect to throw away 50% of what you buy. Do not buy peas with dry or discoloured pods. Fresh peas should be used as quickly as possible while they are young – i.e. not over-ripe – as the sugar in them turns into starch, making them taste insipid. When buying canned peas, descriptions such as 'garden peas', 'best quality' etc are some guide to texture and flavour. The best frozen peas are labelled 'petits pois'.

How to store: keep fresh peas in their pods wrapped in a damp cloth in the salad compartment of your refrigerator for no more than 24 hours.

Preparation and use: shelled peas can be cooked by the conservative method in 10-20 minutes depending on the size and variety; mangetout peas will be ready in 10-15 minutes. Garden peas are good tossed in butter, or in a sauce made with crème

fraîche for special occasions. They go well with spring onions, carrots, sweetcorn and mushrooms and with finely shredded, tender lettuce leaves. Dill, chervil, nutmeg, oregano, parsley, white pepper, fresh mint, sage, chives, basil and a pinch of sugar can be used to season them.

Peppers and Chillies

Peppers - also called capsicums - grow in a variety of colours but are available in the shops mainly in green (unripe), yellow and red. The large yellow and red ones are particularly attractive because of their sweetness and fruity perfume. Chillies, on the other hand, are primarily used for seasoning. They originated from the New World, but are now essential ingredients in the cuisines of almost all hot countries, where they are used in spicy sauces and pastes or to make spice mixtures. They are exported in their fresh, dried or preserved form. Chillies can be green, yellow, orange and red, though the colour is no guide to how hot they are. Nor is size. Some large pointed chillies are mild in flavour, as is the rose-red Hungarian chilli used to make paprika. However, as a rule of thumb, the smaller the chilli the hotter it is likely to be. There are literally hundreds of varieties.

In season: July to November.

Nutritional value: rich in fibre, vitamins A, B_6 and C; also contain protein, fat, carbohydrate, potassium, calcium, phosphorus, magnesium, iron, vitamins E, B_1, B_2, niacin and folic acid; especially low in sodium.

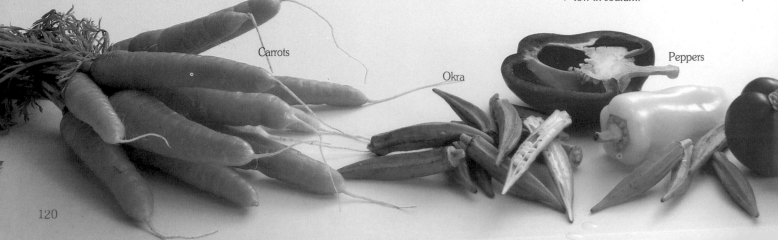

Carrots

Okra

Peppers

About 105kJ/25kcal per 100g/4oz of the edible part.

Advice on buying: look for firm, shiny skins, and avoid any that are split or burst.

How to store: in the salad compartment of your refrigerator for up to 4 days.

Preparation and use: large green peppers are good stuffed, as the stuffing enhances their flavour. It is often a good idea to skin the peppers. To do so, wrap in damp newspaper and place in a hot oven or under a grill and roast until the fine outer skin splits; cool, then rub off the skin. Discard the white pith and seeds of peppers and chillies. In the case of chillies, the seeds are the hottest part. Small amounts of chopped fresh chilli can be added to food as a seasoning. If using as a vegetable, pour boiling water over the prepared chillies and leave to stand 12 to 16 hours before use. Basil, wild marjoram, garlic, marjoram, oregano, paprika and rosemary are suitable as seasoning for mild peppers.

Potatoes

This valuable tuber is cultivated in a bewildering number of varieties, depending on the type of soil and the purpose for which it is used. It is constantly being modified through breeding. As the varieties available vary from one region to another, the names are of less interest than their cooking qualities. Edible potatoes are described as new, early, and main crop. Any of these may have the following cooking qualities:
1. Firm or waxy: salad potatoes

that also roast well; 2. Medium firm: suitable for baked potatoes, boiled potatoes, potato pancakes, and dumplings made from raw grated potato; 3. Floury: popular for vegetable accompaniments and dishes with a sauce or gravy as boiled potatoes, mashed potatoes or potato purée, also suitable for soups and dumplings made of cooked potato.

It is best to keep a supply of two kinds of potato in stock for different uses. The varieties differ in flavour and colour as well as in the way they cook. Try to buy a small quantity of a new variety to start with to try them, then stock up on those you like best.

In season: new potatoes, April to June; earlies, June to August; second earlies, August to September; main crop from September.

Nutritional value: rich in carbohydrate, fibre, potassium, magnesium, vitamins B_6 and C; also contain protein, fat, calcium, phosphorus, iron, iodine, vitamins A, K, B_1, B_2, niacin and folic acid; especially low in sodium. About 295kJ/70kcal per 100g/4oz of the edible part.

Advice on buying: potatoes of the same variety should be more or less even in size. Look for clean, undamaged skins. The potatoes should have no patches of rot or green and should not be sprouting.

How to store: store loose in a basket in a dark, airy place that is as cool as possible, with no special packing, for up to three weeks; never store in the refrigerator or at temperatures below freezing as the starch in the tuber then alters. Only

store maincrop varieties in a dark, unheated area (a shed, garage or cellar) from the end of October. If possible store on a lattice-work or pierced shelf in a well-aired place.

Preparation and use: scrub potatoes under cold running water, removing any green parts and sprouts, as they contain solanin, an alkaloid which is indigestible and bitter. Cooking potatoes in their skins is the best way to preserve the nutritional value. If at all possible, use the water in which the potatoes have been cooked for stock or gravy. Potatoes can be prepared in so many ways and combined with so many other foods, herbs and spices that we will not attempt to list them here. Combined with other vegetables, eggs and curd cheese, potatoes make a very nutritious meal.

Pumpkins, Gourds and Squash

There are several hundred varieties of pumpkin of widely varying shapes and colours. The largest specimens, giant pumpkins, can weigh up to 50kg/112lbs. Apart from these, other varieties which are good as vegetables and are becoming more widely available are bottle-gourd, egg-shaped gourd, common pumpkin, patty-pan squash (a pale-skinned vegetable which resembles the popular image of the flying saucer

in shape) and small summer squashes. These include the chayote, a pale green or yellow pear-shaped variety from South and Central America, also known as chocho or xoxo. Another variety, which looks like a very knobbly cucumber is the bitter gourd, is used extensively in Chinese and Indian cooking.

In season: August to October for locally grown pumpkins. December to March when imported.

Nutritional value: rich in fibre, potassium, vitamin A and folic acid; also contain protein, fat, carbohydrate, calcium, phosphorus, magnesium, iron, vitamins B_1, B_2, niacin and vitamin C; especially low in sodium. About 105kJ/25kcal per 100g/4oz of the edible part.

Advice on buying: the smaller the pumpkin, the more tender and more aromatic the flesh. You can buy cut pumpkin by weight.

How to store: store whole pumpkins at room temperature for 2 weeks; pieces of pumpkin wrapped in aluminum foil can be kept in the salad compartment of the refrigerator for 3 days.

Preparation and use: always peel large pumpkins and discard the seeds. Pumpkins do not have a strong flavour of their own, so when preparing them season them fairly strongly. Suitable seasonings include cayenne, curry powder,

Red cabbage

Brussels sprouts

Beetroot

Parsnip

ginger, garlic, paprika and lemon juice. Sweet-and-sour pickled pumpkin goes well with venison and pork or fillet of beef.

Red cabbage

Red cabbage with its dense structure and blue-green or deep purple gleaming leaves is a delight both to the eye and the palate. It is popular in central Europe.

In season: August to March.

Nutritional value: rich in fibre, potassium, vitamin B_6, folic acid and vitamin C; also contains protein, fat, carbohydrate, calcium, phosphorus, magnesium, iron, iodine, fluorine, vitamins A, B_1, B_2 and niacin; low in sodium. About 125kJ/30kcal per 100g/4oz of the edible part.

Advice on buying: look for crisp, shiny leaves.

How to store: in the salad compartment of your refrigerator for up to 8 days; cut cabbage can be wrapped in foil or clingfilm and stored for up to 3 days; in a dark cool cellar on a duckboard for 1 month.

Preparation and use: red cabbage is best braised. The special flavour is enhanced by the

Sauerkraut

addition of certain spices, a little sweetness and a little acidity – the acidity also creating the brilliant red colour. Red cabbage should be seasoned with an onion with cloves and a bay leaf stuck into it or with caraway seeds, cloves, black pepper, juniper berries and lemon juice. The sweetness can be provided by maple syrup, concentrated pear juice, honey or redcurrant jelly, while the acidity is provided by good red wine vinegar or some red wine. Combined with apples, prunes or chestnuts, red cabbage is delicious with venison and game birds, pork, beef olives, goose, duck and turkey.

Salsify

Salsify are long roots about 3cm/1 $^1/_4$ inches thick with a black or pale brown skin. The delicate white flesh has a flavour similar to that of asparagus, and many gourmets regard it as one of the most subtle vegetables.

In season: November to March.

Nutritional value: rich in carbohydrate, fibre, potassium, magnesium, iron, vitamins E and B_1; also contains protein, fat, calcium, phosphorus, vitamins A, B_2, niacin and vitamin C; especially low in sodium. About 335kJ/80kcal per 100g/4oz of the edible part.

Advice on buying: try to buy firm, unbroken roots that are not forked; you should not be able to bend them.

Asparagus

How to store: tightly wrapped in newspaper in a cool, dry area or in the salad compartment of your refrigerator for up to 3 days.

Preparation and use: Scrub salsify thoroughly under cold running water, peel from the root end to the tip, and place immediately in a mixture of vinegar, flour and water to prevent the vegetable from oxydising. Cut it into pieces of the desired length before cooking. Or place the scrubbed roots in a large saucepan of rapidly boiling water and cook for 20-30 minutes depending on how thick they are. Plunge into cold water, remove the skin, and cook for another 10-20 minutes until they are ready. It is a good idea to wear rubber gloves when preparing salsify because they contain a rust-coloured dye. It is almost impossible to get the stain out of fabric. Salsify taste good in a cream sauce or boiled with breadcrumbs fried in butter over them. Mace, nutmeg, sweet paprika and parsley make suitable seasonings.

Sauerkraut

Sauerkraut is made from finely-shredded white cabbage which is fermented with salt, which makes the sugar contained in the cabbage turn into lactic acid, giving the cabbage its characteristic flavour. For wine-flavoured sauerkraut, wine is added during fermentation. Sauerkraut is exceptionally rich in nutrients, and therefore healthy as well as inexpensive.

In season: all year round - available in delicatessens straight from the barrel, in sealed plastic packets or canned from supermarkets.

Nutritional value: rich in fibre, potassium, vitamins B_6 and C; also contains protein, fat, carbohydrate, sodium, calcium, phosphorus, iron, vitamins A, B_1, B_2 and niacin. About 105kJ/25kcal per 100g/4oz of the edible part.

Advice on buying: when buying pre-packed or canned sauerkraut check the 'best before' date.

How to store: sauerkraut can be kept in the refrigerator for 2 days, once the can or package has been opened. The same goes for sauerkraut from the barrel.

Preparation and use: sauerkraut is best cooked by the conservative method. It is a good idea to reserve a small amount of raw sauerkraut, chop it up finely and add it to the cooked sauerkraut to preserve the maximum nutritional value. Sauerkraut can be combined with sausages, bacon and pork, but can also be used with pineapple, apples, prunes and grapes. With the addition of sparkling, dry white wine, it makes a subtle accompaniment to venison and wildfowl. Cloves, caraway seed, bay leaf, sweet paprika, allspice and juniper berries make suitable seasonings.

Savoy cabbage

Savoy cabbage is a variety of white cabbage with crinkly leaves that do not close tightly. The outside leaves are pale to dark green, while the inside ones are light green to light yellow. The darker the cabbage, the stronger the flavour.

Salsify (scorzonera)

Sorrel

In season: August to January.
Nutritional value: rich in fibre, potassium, folic acid and vitamin C ; also contains protein, fat, carbohydrate, calcium, phosphorus, magnesium, iron, vitamins A, B_1, B_2 and niacin; especially low in sodium.
About 125kJ/30kcal per 100g/4oz of the edible part.
Advice on buying: choose heads that are as firm and compact as possible.
How to store: in the salad compartment of your refrigerator for up to 5 days; in a cool, dark cellar on a duckboard for up to one month.
Preparation and use: savoys with tender, pale leaves are best cooked by the conservative method. Dark-leaved cabbages should first be blanched for 3 minutes, then shredded and cooked in the same way. Any recipe for white cabbage can be used for savoys, though the flavour of the dark cabbage is a little more pungent. Mugwort, coriander, caraway seed, parsley and black pepper can be used as seasonings.

Sorrel

This is a wild meadow plant with tart-tasting, succulent leaves. Recently sorrel has started to be cultivated commercially.
In season: April to August.
Nutritional value: rich in fibre, potassium, magnesium, iron, vitamins A and C ; also contains protein, fat, carbohydrate, calcium and phosphorus; especially low in sodium.
About 105kJ/25kcal per 100g/4oz of the edible part.
Advice on buying: choose succulent green leaves with very tender, crisp stalks; avoid over-

large leaves that are withered or discoloured.
How to store: washed, picked over and wrapped loosely in clingfilm for 1 day in the salad compartment of your refrigerator.
Preparation and use: if you are picking your own sorrel, avoid fields near heavily-used roads and make sure that the grass has not been sprayed with chemicals in the last 3 weeks or so. As a general rule, serve sorrel mixed with other leaf vegetables or salad greens as its flavour is too powerful for it to be enjoyable on its own. However, it is delicious as an omelette ingredient. Sorrel also makes an excellent soup and a sauce for white fish.

Spinach

The leaves of winter spinach which grows outdoors in winter and is not harvested until March or April are coarser in texture, but have an exceptionally good flavour. Summer and autumn spinach have tender leaves which can be used in salads.
In season: March to November.
Nutritional value: rich in fibre, potassium, calcium, magnesium, iron, iodine, fluorine, vitamins A, E, K, B_6, folic acid and vitamin C ; also contains protein, fat, carbohydrate, sodium, phosphorus, vitamins B_1, B_2, and niacin.
About 125kJ/30kcal per 100g/4oz of the edible part.
Advice on buying: the best guide to really fresh spinach is crisp, fresh leaves. If the root is still attached, it should be firm.
How to store: as spinach begins to lose its nutritional value within

hours by evaporation through the surface of the leaves, it should be prepared immediately after being bought, and not stored. If you have to store it, wash the spinach, wrap it in a damp tea-towel and keep in the salad compartment of the refrigerator for a maximum of 12 hours.
Preparation and use: wash spinach thoroughly in several changes of water, and cook gently in the water clinging to the leaves for about 5 minutes, then taste. Never eat reheated spinach; there is a risk that the nitrate it contains may be converted into nitrite which is detrimental to the health, particularly for babies. Yeast flakes, chervil, garlic, lovage, nutmeg, white pepper and allspice are suitable as seasonings.

Swede

This is the vegetable known as neeps in Scotland, and traditionally eaten with haggis. Swedes are related to sugar beet and turnips. The large root is a yellowish-orange colour, and acquires a pleasant bitter-sweet taste when cooked.

In season: October to April.
Nutritional value: rich in fibre, calcium, vitamin B_6, folic acid and vitamin C ; also contains protein, fat, carbohydrate, potassium, phosphorus, iron, fluorine, vitamins A, B_1, B_2 and niacin; especially low in sodium.
About 190kJ/45kcal per 100g/4oz of the edible part.
Advice on buying: look for firm, undamaged roots with no rotten areas or discoloration; pick smaller swedes if possible as they are more tender and there is less waste.
How to store: in the salad compartment of your refrigerator for up to 2 weeks; cut swede wrapped in clingfilm for up to 1 week.
Preparation and use: discard the root and any leaves on top, and cut away a thick layer of peel to reveal the light-coloured flesh. Dice, and boil for 40-50 minutes or until tender, or cook by the conservative method. Combine swede with potatoes, leeks, carrots and celeriac; this makes a particularly tasty stew. Mashed swede with butter and cream is a subtle accompaniment to roast pork or lamb. Nutmeg, mugwort,

Celery

Spinach

Tomatoes

Vegetables from A to Z

fennel seeds, ginger, caraway seeds, paprika, white pepper, parsley, chives and wormwood are good as seasonings.

Sweetcorn, Corn-on-the-cob

True sweetcorn can be bought canned or frozen and is grown in America. Corn-on-the-cob is grown in the south of England and is sold fresh. Miniature sweetcorn, once only used in Chinese cooking, is now on the market.

In season: Canned sweetcorn all year round. Corn on the cob, September to October.

Nutritional value: rich in carbohydrate, fibre, potassium, phosphorus, magnesium, vitamins A, B_6, folic acid and pantothenic acid; also contains protein, fat, calcium, vitamins E, B_1, B_2 and C; especially low in sodium. About 440kJ/105kcal per 100g/4oz of the edible part.

Advice on buying: the grains of freshly picked cobs should squirt a whitish sap when scratched with the fingernail. You can check this through cling film or by peeling back the protective green leaves. When buying canned corn, note the 'best before' date.

How to store: ideally, not at all. The quicker you cook sweetcorn after picking, the better. If you have to store it, do so for no more than 2 days in the salad compartment of your refrigerator, as the sugar in the corn then converts into starch, impairing the flavour.

Preparation and use: remove the protective green leaves and silky threads from fresh cobs if necessary. Miniature sweetcorn and even baby cobs are best simply grilled or stir-fried and served with fresh or browned butter. Cobs with well developed grains should be boiled in salted water for 20-30 minutes and served with melted butter. Canned sweetcorn is top quality and is suitable for salads or as a vegetable. Miniature sweetcorn go very well in a stir-fry with mange-tout, Chinese mushrooms and beansprouts. Cayenne, curry powder, paprika and white pepper are suitable spices for seasoning.

Sweet Potatoes

Sweet potatoes, also known as yams, are not related to potatoes biologically. They are the bulbous roots of a type of Morning Glory that grows in warm climates, and are imported. There are varieties with white, yellow and red flesh, the yellow having the best flavour. The yellow-fleshed sweet potatoes are called yams in the United States, and the name is sometimes used over here. When boiled they are similar in texture to floury potatoes, but fried or baked they become waxy or even sticky.

In season: all year round.

Nutritional value: rich in carbohydrate, fibre, potassium, magnesium, iron, vitamins A, B6 and pantothenic acid; also contain protein, fat, calcium, phosphorus, vitamins B_1, B_2, and C; especially low in sodium. About 400kJ/95kcal per 100g/4oz of the edible part.

Advice on buying: look for firm roots with no bad spots, preferably select smallish sweet potatoes with a point at each end.

How to store: in a dry, cool place for up to 2 weeks; not in the refrigerator.

Preparation and use: the best way to cook them is to boil them unpeeled, like potatoes in their skins, for 20-30 minutes depending on their size, then proceed with your recipe. Their sweet individual flavour is accentuated by a honey glaze, powdered or fresh grated ginger or grated orange peel. With these seasonings, sweet potatoes make a particularly good accompaniment for venison, wildfowl and roast pork. Liberally seasoned with cayenne, paprika or rosemary they are good in casseroles or savoury bakes, or can be served alone.The delicate flavour of white-fleshed sweet potatoes makes them a good susbstitute for chestnuts.

Swiss Chard

Swiss chard is very like spinach, but the leaves are a little tougher and it has a pleasantly acrid flavour. It can be used as a green vegetable until the stems are fully grown. At this point, the sturdy stems and ribs are treated and cooked like asparagus while the leaves and the stems which are still tender can be cooked by the conservative method in just a few minutes.

In season: July to September.

Nutritional value: rich in fibre, potassium, calcium, iron, vitamins A, B_2, folic acid and vitamin C ; also contains protein, fat, carbohydrate, sodium, phosphorus, vitamins B_1 and niacin. About 105kJ/25kcal per 100g/4oz of the edible part.

Advice on buying: as with spinach, buy Swiss chard as fresh as possible. Crisp stems and fresh leaves without withered and discoloured areas indicate freshness.

How to store: Swiss chard quickly loses its valuable vitamins when stored. It is best to use it immediately. If it has to be kept for a little while, pick it over, wash it and wrap in a damp cloth, and keep for no more than 12 hours in the salad compartment of your refrigerator.

Preparation and use: All recipes using spinach can be successfully adapted for Swiss chard. Only cook the leaves and stems together when they are very young. Strip the coarse leaves off the fully grown stems, and add just a small quantity of the chopped leaves during the last 5 minutes of cooking. The stems are cooked like asparagus and taste best in a cream sauce or prepared in the Polish style (page 000). Garlic, lovage, parsley, white pepper and lemon juice are suitable seasonings.

White cabbage

Turnips

Jerusalem artichokes

Tomatoes

Round tomatoes of immaculate appearance are available throughout the year, cultivated under glass. However, those grown in the open taste best. Beefsteak tomatoes are best for vegetable dishes and stuffing. The longer plum tomatoes from Italy are suitable for cooking by the conservative method or grilling. The little cherry or salad tomatoes are particularly thin-skinned and full of flavour. Home-grown, green tomatoes are very good in preserves or as a sweet pie filling.

In season: July to September.

Nutritional value: rich in fibre, potassium, magnesium, vitamins A, K, folic acid and vitamin C; also contain protein, fat, carbohydrate, calcium, phosphorus, iron, iodine, fluorine, vitamins B_1 and B_2; especially low in sodium. About 85kJ/20kcal per 100g/4oz of the edible part.

Advice on buying: look for tomatoes that have smooth, unbroken skins and are evenly ripened but not too soft.

How to store: at room temperature in as dark a place as possible for 5 days. Partly green tomatoes will ripen in this time.

Preparation and use: remove green areas and a wedge from the stalk end - the green parts contain solanin, a toxin. For elegant salads and delicate vegetable dishes, tomatoes should be skinned and seeded. Tomatoes combine well with onions and/or cheese, particularly mozarella. Basil, tarragon, garlic, parsley, white or black pepper, rosemary, sage, chives and thyme all make good seasonings.

Turnips

There are several varieties of white turnip, ranging from long to round in shape and white, yellow and pale brown in colour. The skin is whitish with a purplish tinge at the stem end. The flesh of the white turnip is tender, with a mild and pleasantly distinctive flavour.

In season: May, and July to September.

Nutritional value: rich in fibre, calcium, folic acid and vitamin C; also contain protein, fat, carbohydrate, sodium, potassium, phosphorus, magnesium, iron, vitamins B_1, B_2 and niacin. About 85kJ/20kcal per 100g/4oz of the edible part.

Advice on buying: look for firm, unblemished roots; the size is no guide to the quality.

How to store: in the salad compartment of your refrigerator for up to 3 days.

Preparation and use: top and tail the turnips and scrub under running water, scrape or peel, then proceed according to the recipe. Young turnips are delicious tossed in a caramelised sugar and butter glaze, or served in a butter sauce. Larger round turnips can be stuffed. White turnips combine well with chervil, nutmeg, parsley, white pepper, salad burnet, shallots, mustard and wormwood.

White Cabbage

White (or Dutch) cabbage is one of the finest varieties with a mild flavour and a crisp, but tender texture. Its cheapness belies its value. Early white cabbage is still quite green; later heads suitable for storing have tightly packed, pale yellow leaves with a light waxy coating.

In season: August to September but, because it stores well, available until March.

Nutritional value: rich in fibre, magnesium, vitamins K and C; also contains protein, fat, carbohydrate, potassium, calcium, phosphorus, iron, iodine, fluorine, vitamins A, B_1, B_2 and niacin; especially low in sodium. About 105kJ/25kcal per 100g/4oz of the edible part.

Advice on buying: look for tight, compact heads.

How to store: in the salad compartment of your refrigerator for 1 week; in a cool, dark cellar on a lattice-work shelf for up to 2 months.

Preparation and use: white cabbage is best braised. It combines particularly well with fresh beans, carrots, leeks, celeriac and onions, and is a good accompaniment for pork, mutton, lamb, smoked sausage and bacon.

Caraway seeds are particularly good as seasoning, but mugwort, borage, coriander, lovage, bay leaves, nutmeg, parsley, white pepper and chives are also good.

> kJ = kilojoules
> kcal = kilocalories; in every case all the data relating to nutritional value refer to 100g/4oz of the edible part of the raw vegetable.

Savoy cabbage

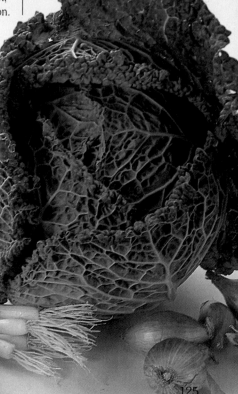

Courgettes

Onions

Index

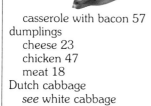

Index

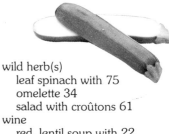